With best wishes
and sincere appreciation
for your kindness

Henry McKenzie

fundamentals
the church needs

BY henry mckenzie

Pastor Emeritus, College Presbyterian Church

Murray, Kentucky

International Standard Book Number 0-8418-4583-2
Library of Congress Catalog Card Number 70-148557
Copyright © 1970, The University Press

Printed in the United States of America
THE UNIVERSITY PRESS
Wolfe City, Texas 75496

To

Dorothy Jean, Ian and Norma,
Our grandchildren, geographically far away but
near the hearts of their grandparents and
always in their prayers.

"The youth who will rule tomorrow is the youth who today is storing up resources of knowledge and wisdom, of self-reliance and courage.". . .

"Heroic leaders and guides have been as unique in their spiritual faith as in their mental gifts. Lift up your ideals and rise to their level. Strengthen faith, the faith that brings fellowship with the good and great among men, with the One Who is the greatest, the Divine Christ, our Savior and Example; and with God, the Author of character, and the Finisher Who crowns the life with enduring strength and beauty."

—Newell Dwight Hillis

Foreword

This book is written for laymen and ministers who are interested in the mental turmoil of the church. Let us admit that both the laity and clergy often find it difficult, if not impossible, to accept the Christian tradition. Many minds have always found it impossible to accept the ecclesiastical interpretation of Christianity. In the last few decades under the influence of modern science, historical criticism, rationalistic philosophy, and Biblical higher criticism, many have found it impossible to accept traditional Christianity. The intellectual culture of today finds the doctrines of the church alien to its thinking. It is toward this difficulty the basic theological themes, outlined by the church, are directed in this volume.

Those of us who defend and live and work for the church are endeavoring to bring firm and consistent convictions that will meet the essential needs in this changing world. The convictions must be vital and vitalizing and must be expressed without fear or prejudice. The ecclesiastical authority of past years will not suffice. All truth is not taken to the laboratory. The church must express facts that are credible to the intellect and inspiring to the soul. The whole personality must be involved, with mind, heart, will, soul, equally balanced and recompensed—"What is the breadth and length and depth and height?"—Ephesians 3:18. It is evident that the church cannot be all things to all people, however, we may attempt the ideal. A French wit said, "We cannot do with the church, and we cannot do without it." Contrary to many of our skeptics decrying the weaknesses and limitations of the church, they cannot offer an institution or organization upholding higher ethical values or finer spiritual ideals. The church still holds the Light of the world and the salt of the earth in its Gospel.

The title of the book has been suggested by college professors in the congregation. "Fundamentals The Church

Needs," indicates the spirit rather than the contents. The sermons were presented to those in theological ferment, concurrently with a desire to remain with the church. They intelligently felt the problems and were interested enough to want to think them through. They assured me they were not willing to accept "Thus saith the Lord," and fall into the arms of traditional authority. This is hopeful for the Christian church—when men teaching and supervising automation, technology, atomic energy, jet propulsion, and space travel, demand the church to be relevant to the highest and best that has been said and done in the world. The church that has preached, in season and out, the Kingdom of God, has been with the aristocracy of the intellect. In this company, I have tried to be articulate and the sermons which follow are closely related to their philosophy of religion. Together we were meeting the demands of the church.

It is already evident that my purpose is to meet the current needs of the church and I do so without striving for philosophic profundity or theological subtlety. The sermons are written as they are spoken from brief outlines. There is no attempt at criticism or an attack on church trivialities and namby-pamby creedal impotence, but rather to affirm the fundamentals and give priority to the basic principles of Christianity. Carlyle says, "A man's faith does not consist in what he does not believe." If there is anywhere in the sermons implied demolition, it is done to give greater affirmation to the Christian faith. If it tears down, it is to build more worthily.

It is the author's belief that the minister of Christ is to declare only sovereign principles in order to coordinate the entire church program. Every sermon emphasizes the goodness of life and the dignity of man. If we do not apply our religion, it is obviously ineffective. You will find every sermon contending truth is absolute, but our understanding of it must constantly change. The paradox I find in the church is its plea for peace at the expense of truth. It offers self-attainment at the expense of happiness. It offers mind at the expense of heart.

In protestantism we find differences because of our democratic governments and the priesthood of believers. These sermons do not attempt to maintain absolute unity or uniformity in the church for it is not utopian. No sermon is infallible, no preacher is inerrant, and no church is perfect. The well-balanced pulpiteer will not limit his expositions to either dogma or ethics, but will equally emphasize creeds with deeds, personal salvation with social service, the supernatural with the human, and his priestly duties with his prophetic messages.

The reader will, no doubt, detect the author's conversion from humanism to mysticism. There will be evidence of a spiritual pilgrimage from the social to the religious, from ethical conduct to Christian faith, and from the anthropocentric philosophy to the theocentric. I have gone with Amos and witnessed the word "Righteousness" grow until it becomes as vast as the character of God. With Hosea, I have watched the word "Love" grow until it becomes as exhaustless as the heart of God. I have endeavored to give humanism wings of inspiration. Now I know, and here declare, that the infinite speaks to the finite; and the eternal penetrates the temporal. Categorically, you will find in every chapter, faith transcending the human. I am, however, pragmatic enough to contend that it is not the church that makes good men, but that good men make the church.

The goal in twenty sermons is to bring and keep the unity of spirit in the bond of peace. Throughout this volume, belief in the importance of thought and respect for the personalities and convictions of others are upheld. There is no claim to absolute truth. There is absolute belief, however, in the constructive principle of love as contrasted with evil, hatred, and hypocrisy. The church must give the peace that the world cannot give nor take away. There must be cooperation rather than argument and hope rather than fear. The stress must be laid upon principles rather than policies, and upon duties rather than rights. Salvation must be attained here as well as hereafter. The messages must not only be timely, but also timeless, because they are Christ-centered.

My sincere desire is to have laymen and preachers of all denominations examine the contents of this book and feel that Christ calls each of us to grow and help others to grow toward wisdom revealed in Christ. These are the Fundamentals The Church Needs.

Contents

FUNDAMENTALS
THE CHURCH NEEDS

THE GENERATION GAP

Text: "Prove all things; hold fast to that which is good."

—I Thessalonians 5:21

Shakespeare wrote of the seven ages of man and by his genius made his classification permanent in our thought. Human life, as we know it, really encompasses not more than three generations at any one time: youth, maturity, and age. It is possible to subdivide the classifications, such as young adults and adults. At this period we have violence and protest songs of the second generation. In the news media we hear that the future rests with them. Nevertheless, on the strong, resolute, stern men of middle age rest the great responsibilities of leadership and ultimate control. The heat and enthusiasm cannot displace reason, balance, experience, and mature judgment.

Our primary task is to take a long hard look ahead. Into the hands of college youths will fall full power for tomorrow. They vote and the radical's vote is equal to that of the philosopher. It is commonplace to say that we are giving them the equipment and potential power for greatness. Regardless of the turmoil and divisions in race, color, and creed, this age will stand out as a mountain peak above the plains of the mediocre. It is an age that has converged the forces of the centuries which have gathered strength for this inevitable conflict. We have revitalized our ideals and institutions to bring in this new civilization we call the atomic age.

With automation, technology, and nuclear energy, we have not overcome our heritage of pagan practices. Science, philosophy, and religion have not captivated imagination; and morality has not been exercised—witness the war in Viet Nam, starvation in Biafra, the middle east building armies and

1

military hardware, and civilians slaughtered by the hundreds, not to mention the tremendous increase in crime, drugs, and pornography. The savage of yesteryear cannot teach us a small per cent of modern treachery. Can we foretell when pagan practices will give way to idealism and ethical culture with Christian emphasis?

The path of the future leads either up or down. Many believe that a spiritually exhausted humanity will collapse. Still others believe that the confused, perplexed upheaval will lead to a nobler era; out of confusion will come order, out of chaos will come cosmos. If I interpret the Gospel aright, in the providence of God, the path will lead to the heights. It will be upward because at the heart of the universe is righteousness. The dice are loaded and God is in the heavens. This does not detract from the duty of maturity to sacrifice and continue making adjustments. We have conscripted the teen-agers to war; we have given them the world of science that enables man to walk on the moon, and we have made materialism the goal of life. Materialism is the god of plenty rather than of quality. The old order must change lest one good custom corrupt the world.

Let us take a pragmatic view of things as they are. We mention foreign policy and conclude it is war, or else. We have black consciousness which is "black power" and Social Security which is part poverty and slums. In this maze of pandemonium the young adult says, "The folks do not understand us." The parents say, "We do not know where these young people are coming out." Youth and age are involved and each shares responsibility for they are both participants.

In mid-ocean where currents meet, there are troubled waters. Two years ago on Vancouver Island the bus driver stopped and pointed to merging currents coming from opposite directions. He explained, "More ships have been lost down at that junction than on all the western coast." The generations meet, one looking to the past and the other to the future—one pushes from behind and the other crowds for the front—one is directing from experience and the other directing from anticipation. The two philosophies trying to guide the ship of life meet with disaster.

Our text has the only answer which I know: "Prove all things; hold fast to that which is good." Both generations want to go to the heights but in different directions. The old is not all bad and the new is not all good. We need acceleration and we need brakes. My American Legion Magazine carried a cartoon. It was the baseball homecoming annual event. A boy slid home in the ninth inning to win the game for the cheering citizens, a hero. In the process of winning, he tore his trousers. At home, his belaboring father punished him. The boy was in a quandary: to the community a hero, and at home a villain—the difference in values of age and youth.

This generation gap is an eternal problem. Psychologically, age is conservative and youth radical. Age is cautious and youth daring. Age has direction and youth energy. Age has too many memories and youth too few. Age has too little time ahead and youth has too little time behind. Age saves its resources and youth spends excessively. A father and son climbing a mountain stop to rest. The father says, "See how far we have come," and the son says, "See how far we have to go."

Without the old we could not have the new. At one time the old was new. Galileo's primitive glass made possible the Wilson observatory. Newton's gravitation made possible Einstein's relativity. Watts' steam kettle made possible the railroad. Gutenberg's movable type made possible modern education. We cannot make progress without turning to the past. Concurrently we have to hold on and let go. We let go of Judaism to get Christianity; of Romanism to get protestantism; of the dark ages to get the renaissance; of the divine right of kings to get democracy; of ancient creeds to get ethical religion, and we have to let go of tradition to get progress. Letting go is both an asset and a liability, a privilege with responsibility.

We have let go of our puritanical morals and consequently we have sex freedom, crowded jails, street violence, divorce and social indifference. We have let go of much of our spiritual inheritance and we have material prosperity with moral collapse. France let go of the Bourbon monarchy and they let go of their government. They wanted freedom, prosperity, and peace; but they found confusion and revolution called "the reign of terror." The child lets go of the old toy of value for the new trinket. Progress can only come by proving and discarding and holding on to the proven worth. To differ in opinion is inevitable, but for youth and maturity to attack one another has retarded progress in every age. It is a paradox that disagreement has made for progress. It has also led to persecution and inquisitions. Philosophy teaches that life is a battlefield and youth and age are not alone in the struggle. Think of the rural and city antagonisms, capital and labor, the fundamentalism and modernism which divided the church for years. Ethical problems take the front page of our daily papers. We live in an age of divided interests.

No one brought more controversy than Christ. All the forces of His day, including the state, synagogue, and society, called Him a radical. They demanded the heretic be crucified. His ideas were nailed to the hearts of men and for nineteen centuries have been "the faith once delivered to the saints," and have been the motivation for the building of the Kingdom in today's world. The altar versus the pulpit, uniformity versus variations, independence versus establishments—the only answer is, "Prove all things, hold fast to that which is good." A sin of age is the unwillingness to examine and experiment; the sin of youth is their unwillingness to give consideration to practices and principles tried and not found wanting.

In defense of age, and I speak as a modern progressive, I do not know of one scholar who believes the world will ever be the same after the dissensions of this decade. Age believes the new social order must come from youth. It will require organization, administration and spiritualization. The new regime must have more than dissent against establishment; it must have wisdom and skill. The problems of the future will not be solved by marches, but rather by reflection. We must make our youth aware that virtues may become vices. They have rights, but not without duties. They have privileges, but not without responsibilities.

In this life of paradoxes where youth is involved, they have questions that demand answers. I say to them, "Attend church on the Sabbath." I have had Westminster Fellowship college students say, "When I go home, I hear about the sun standing still, dry sticks becoming serpents, cities let down out of the sky, and donkeys talking. Frankly, I can't take it. Here in the University we are taught law and ethics and logic." I have given them an illustration, with limitations, but with some merit for consideration: men have traveled continents, oceans, and the heavens with the aid of one instrument, the compass. It began under Henry II in England, in 1154. Seeking direction, men would touch a needle to a bit of magnetic iron and the needle would whirl and infallibly point to the north. This was an authority, an absolute law of the universe. Nearly two thousand years ago a small group of people, perplexed, confused, began to follow Him Who said, "I am the way, the truth, and the life." Here was a divine compass. Following, they found the abundant life. I say to youth, "It is not science, but the character of the people who apply the science." Alfred the Great said, "Power is never a good, except he is good that has it." Science is your study, but if it saves without character, it also kills. Christ made character for age and youth supreme. Here is a progressive, a Galilean youth living where the action is. He is the wisest among the teachers; the noblest among the reformers; the purest among the holy and the saintliest among the martyrs.

He fills the generation gap. His character is the final test of personality, and his views are the final test of all truth. He is not only timely but timeless. He has never taken a backward step, never reversed a decision, never recalled a single word. He never hesitated in uncertainty, he has always been in advance. His words are eternal, He is never afraid of tomorrow. His truth is deathless as His righteousness is boundless.

This is the challenge to this generation—Prove all things. Let go of the inferior. Hold fast to the good. Here is One Who is the same, yesterday, today, and forever.

"Thou art the science and the love,
Of men through ages long since dust.
Their hard won wisdom, slowly grown,
Came down to us a sacred trust.

Ours for the present to increase
Ours for the future and its care,
A heritage of growing light;
To live, transmit and greatly share."

(My notebook carries these lines, and I know not the author.)

RELIGION FOR THE ADULT MIND

Text: "When I was a child, I thought as a child . . . . when I
became a man I put away childish things."
—I Corinthians 13:11

Few things are more fascinating than the changing
moods, uncertainties, and unreasonableness of children.
Without real cause, they can go from laughter to tears. They
are creatures of impulse, often satisfied with little things and
resentful of big ones. They live in a world of fables, fancies,
fairies, and make-believe. Their dolls are given human
attributes. They love them, dress them, punish them, and
nurse them. Children are animists, believing that all life is
produced by a spiritual force that is separated from matter.
Their toys have souls. Walt Disney's fairy land and his
mystical characters are real! Tell children of the giant-killer,
or Alice in Wonderland, or Peter Pan in Never-Never Land,
and they will say, "Tell me more."

Children are fascinating, affectionate, enchanting, and
adorable. We would not have them any other way. With
mixed emotions, we say the law of life will change all of this.
They will outgrow the imaginary for the actual, the mystical
for the verifiable, the fantastic for the real, and the
illusionary for the actual. If they fail in this, the childlikeness
becomes childishness. Failure to make this transition
becomes pathological—adults in years and children in emotional development, like Peter Pan who never grew up. We
have, in every sphere of life, adolescent adults who accept the
mythical and magical without reflection or without gaining
analysis; fairies that never lose their wings and wands;
Cinderella in the pumpkin coach is going to the ball. Much of
mythology still exists in religious circles. Emotional religion
is more pertinent than the rational.

7

The adult mind retains its childish curiosity but continues to explore and scrutinize every opinion, custom, tradition, and belief! Nothing remains unexamined. All popular beliefs are critically questioned and re-examined. It is true that modern anthropology has unearthed the characteristic beliefs of primitive man and many myths have become intelligible. Nevertheless, reason must supplant mythology with knowledge. It is true, the whole system of hopes and fears, sanctions, and taboos which the traditional view of the world had fostered, protested against a rational investigation. The adult mind has become aware of the nature of myth and legend. Religious dogma, in the same way, will be examined as to origin, development and results. Profound questions must have profound answers.

When we put away childish things, we ask questions. I have received many inquiries from students, asking: "Do we have to believe that the serpent spoke to Eve, and if the serpent strikes it will not kill? Did woman come from Adam's rib? Why does it say that Joshua had the sun to stand still? Did Solomon have seven hundred wives and three hundred prostitutes? Was Noah five hundred years old when Shem, Ham and Japheth were born? Did Nebuchadnezzar eat grass like an ox for seven years?" On and on these questions were asked by maturing minds, to quote: "Our church says doubt is dangerous and destructive. How can we think if we do not doubt? Isn't it true that knowledge has come to us because someone, somewhere, sometime, asked questions?"

It is commonplace to say that the conservatives today are following the ultra-radicals of yesterday. A man says, "I believe like my father." The difficulty is, the father did not believe like his grandfather or we would be back in fetishism, magic, shamanism, human sacrifice and totemism. Somewhere along the line there had to be progressives, nonconformists, and heretics. Progress can only come by questioning the status quo. Without examination and rebellion we would have stagnation and ultimate death. We can never say, "This is final—this is absolute—this is infallible—this is perfection, there is no need of further inquiry." How true: "The old order changes lest one good custom should corrupt the world." We do not hold an idea because it is old, or because it is widely held. We hold it because it is true. The old is not always bad, the new is not always good. Searching for truth requires the matured mind. It is free from the fear of new facts; free from arbitrarily imposed authority; free from the tyranny of circumstances; free from the dictates of cults, crowds, and creeds. Man is free to grow.

Man has religiously moved out of shamanism into polytheism, then into henotheism, then into monotheism, then into Judaism, then into Christianity. Man has questioned every taboo, social practice, and conventional morality, believing that knowing the truth he would be free. He demanded scientific proof and added that he wanted science in his religion as he wanted religion in his science. He said, "Religion must be intellectually respectable." It is true that in the past science looked upon religion with apprehension and religion looked upon science with distrust. Today the matured mind has real science and rational religion in quest of additional truths.

The chief glory of man is that he is a thinking being. This is what constitutes his "divine image." It is true in all mechanical creation that man is the most delicate and complex being. He is the masterpiece of God's creative genius, but the "divine image" is man's mental and moral faculties. David's description is understood:

"Thou hast made him but little lower than God,
And crowned him with glory and honor."

It is man's nature to think, reason, and purpose. The ministry of Jesus includes His ethical restrictions: "The old says, but I say unto you." He knew the greatest power in the world is not in physical nature but in man's mind. Modern man, with his automation and technology, with steam, electricity, radium, and nuclear energy, has harnessed nature and has developed ability to penetrate its deepest mystery and utilize its hidden secrets. Science is the thought of God written into the world. It is thinking God's thoughts after Him. All of nature is thought materialized. Government is thought organized into law for well being. Art is thought thrown on the canvas, chiseled in marble or sung in oratorio. Religion is thought embodied in developing creeds tested by experience. Christianity is thought in the Divine Mind of the Son of God.

The adult mind must learn to stretch the finite world into an infinite universe; be able to see the growth from the protozoan to the mind of Plato; from the unicellular organism into the mind of Einstein; and the anthropos (man, the upward looking one) into the image of God. "Some call it evolution and others call it God." This is the adult mind attaining self-realization. It evolves and unfolds all the possibilities in man. The world could see a business man, cheating his own race and kind, but Christ could see in Matthew, an apostle and builder of the Kingdom of righteousness. John Ruskin was more than a man of letters, he was an amateur chemist. He took home a cup of muddy water to analyze. He found four ingredients: sand, clay, carbon, water. He thought of their potentials. The sand became a sapphire; the clay an opal; the carbon, a diamond; the water a snowflake. To the matured mind there are two opposite poles, the actual and the possible, the real and the ideal, what is and what can be, today's substance and tomorrow's transcendence. Christ said, "It is the power *to become!*"

The matured mind knows that the mounting material outputs and our increasing technical know-how have not added to our moral stature. The abundance of things coming from science has not produced the abundant life. The highest standard of living has not produced the highest standard of happiness. Our proud atomic age is still an age of aspirin and ulcers. The scientific mind does not guarantee goodness. A doctoral degree may be given to a moron without a degree of decency. John Dewey, America's foremost teacher, said,

"Our science of human nature, in comparison with physical sciences, is rudimentary." Einstein, whose mind embraced a boundless universe with mathematical equations, was asked to take the presidency of the University of Israel. He replied, "I have neither the natural ability nor experience to deal with human beings."

We need the matured mind in Religion. To save us from fanaticism and credulity, we need to think straight, critically, independently, and constructively. We have already contended that morality outdistanced by intellect is dangerous. We need knowledge but also wisdom in control. I do not believe in an infallible science any more than I believe in an infallible religion. I cannot go along with Canon Streeter's book, "Reality." He says, "Science is concerned solely with the measurable, religion solely with values." I believe the world is one. God is the Author of both measure and values. The mind that puts away childish things says: "If there is darkness, let there be light; if bondage, let there be freedom; if anguish, let there be healing; and if there is sin, let there be righteousness." The Christian is commissioned to *see clearly, think honestly, live victoriously* and *serve unselfishly*. This is maturity! It is remembering that knowledge needs conscience and conscience needs knowledge. Knowledge must develop into wisdom. The great commandment, Christ said, is to "Love God with *all* your mind." Paul wrote, "Whatsoever things are true and honorable and just and pure and lovely, think on these things." Then, and then only, do we put away childish things. Let us enter the full realization of George Eliot's noble dream:

"Oh, may I join the choir invisible
Of those immortal dead who live again
In minds made better by their presence; live
In pulses stirred to generosity,
In deeds of daring rectitude, in scorn
Of miserable aims that end with self;
In thoughts that pierce the night like stars,
And with their wild persistence urge men's search
To vaster issues."

THE PROPHETIC VOICE AND ITS ADVENTURE

Text: "How shall they hear without a preacher?"
—Romans 10:14

The primary task in life is to bring spiritual health, happiness, and courage into the lives of people. Whatever our vocation may be and regardless of the nature of our cultural background, our lives are failures unless, in some manner, they radiate light and strength in the community, unless they improve the tone of life and increase the stamina within their sphere of influence. We are all called upon to be good Samaritans and to give counsel or listen sympathetically to friends who are perplexed or harassed by life. We are to bear witness to the truth, even when it brings persecution or social discrimination against us.

The ministry, as a profession, represents or should represent an extraordinary interest in people and a passionate devotion to truth. It is more to the minister than a means of livelihood or an attempt to get favoritism from the community. He is one who has felt the need of giving his whole life to the Kingdom. He has a dedicated purpose to invest all his energy and his intelligence in his preaching and in the art of worship that will ultimately bring Christian character to his people. He is consecrated to the Highest Good, so is happily compelled to lead in advance, however humble his leadership may be, toward a larger realization of what we call the Gospel. He specializes in that attestation and in those services which are rendered frequently by the laity. The preacher has occasion to espouse some ideal cause that is vital to life and he is to exhort both by precept and example; to put into requisition the contents of the Kingdom of righteousness.

The function of the ministry from age to age remains essentially unchanged. At best, the minister is a prophet and a servant. The spiritual needs of individuals are not altered with the centuries. Human nature is basically the same regardless of time or place. The ancient prophets were in harmony with modern apostolic calling. They gave moral and spiritual commandments which today's pulpiteer must communicate to his congregation; while his personal ministry must sometimes rebuke, but more often bring comfort and light. His privileges are responsibilities, so he should be doubly sensitive to human wants, with a depth of soul and breadth of compassion that are not generally manifested by people.

Such a mission will, of course, bring discouragements. The very nature of an ideal, (and the realm of ideals is a paramount concern to religion and cannot easily be attained) and the fulfilling of his commission humbles one in the pursuit to "be perfect as your Father in heaven is perfect." Phillips Brooks declared that for a minister to feel equal to his work is a dangerous sign. It indicates he does not know what his work is, or that he thinks too highly of himself, or his job, or both. There are antidotes for the minister's moments of depression. They include: the conviction that the work he is endeavoring to do is the most important thing in the world; that faith and that sense of mission which, regardless of consequences, patiently and perseveringly pursue great ends; the knowledge which informs a man that anything as fundamental and important as Christianity can never be defeated and that work in its behalf can never be futile; that spiritual affinity by which a man is concerned not with tangible evidence of the fruit of his labor, but by which he is made responsible only to his conscience and his God. A Christian minister must work with optimism and a charitable disposition, and, whether he wears laurels or thorns, in the end, he labors with Him Who "overcomes the world."

The preacher in the pulpit must be convinced beyond a doubt that his fundamental duty is "Feed My sheep." Then his preaching will be more effective than all the intellectual hypotheses and logical arguments. Truth which relates to the teachings and life of Christ must be humanized by passing through the human mind, and when communicated powerfully, it always comes to us draped in imagination, reason, and moral feelings. The Gospel of Christ, word for word, is of no consequence when spoken by one who does not believe it in his heart and soul. Preaching is the impartation of truth through personality. The personality must, therefore, be characterized by such sincerity and earnestness as will provide an appropriate vehicle for the message that it bears. The interpretation the minister incarnates to translate must be spiritually disciplined and morally strong. The first and final requirement of his pulpit work is that the minister desires to serve God and man; to speak the truth and to uplift his brethren, he must be absolutely honest and definitely sincere.

I have in my library the "Yale Lectures on Preaching." Almost weekly I make a spiritual pilgrimage to their experienced teachings. In addition, I have the works of great pulpiteers who have influenced me in my work. Preaching is not only vocation but my avocation. "Woe is me if I preach not the Gospel." I said that preaching is truth through personality. It must be Christ-centered. Someone has said it is both an art and an incarnation. I thank god I have listened to and read the sermons of poetic Frederick Shannon and a personal visit with him netted me the first volume he received from the printer of his book, "The Country Faith." He gave me more than the inscribed "good wishes" in his book; he gave me a dream, a vision. He and other former pastors of Central Church, Chicago, gave me the edict to preach, but the pledge "to bring good tidings of good, that publisheth salvation; that saith unto Zion, 'Thy God reigneth' "; another pulpit genius, Frank Gunsaulus, the philosophical builder of a city with its technical institute and art museum; the preacher's preacher, Newell Dwight Hillis, the encyclopedic master of literature, who trusted the predestinated dominion of ideas, and presented them without an equal. Incidentally, my older son bears the name, Hillis, born at the time of Newell Dwight's death. There are numbers of other masters of the pulpit who have greatly influenced my thinking and practices. I heard the masterful genius of my own pastor, Charles F. Wishart, in Second Church, Chicago, with his theological dialectics; the ethical preacher of technical theoretical problems, Henry Churchill King—I had the pleasure of traveling with and introducing him to the Marines in the A.E.F.; masters like Joseph Fort Newton and S. Parkes Cadman. In class, there was the inspirational Henry S. Coffin, and the pastoral theologian, without peer, Cleland B. McAfee. Today I owe them a sense of debt I can never pay. May their teachings and example abide in the libraries of preachers. These Christian preachers and many others believed the Gospel, believed in the triumph of goodness, for they made pessimism a form of vulgar atheism.

Materialism has drained the soul of inspiration and secularism is in the saddle. Sunday after Sunday I enter the pulpit mindful of the majestic fraternity to which I belong; what romantic traditions surround me; and the conscious need of the truth to be preached; the limitations I have, to be equal to the task. I know the sermon is my own experience. Newman said, "Nothing anonymous will preach." In homiletics we were taught that the sermon is a symphony of the spirit. We call upon knowledge. A shallow spirit will produce a shallow sermon. The primary preparation of a sermon is the culture of the inner life. Carlyle said, "I go to church to learn about God; not hearsay, but to hear what the preacher knows about God." Today, our generation demands reality. This is a pragmatic age. Spiritual experience is a blend of discovery, aspiration, realization, and ideal. A man said, "I go to church to hear sermons that make religion an everyday matter and bring it down to earth." His wife said, "That is why I go to another church where it is not a matter and thing of earth, I want a far-off horizon."

Out of nearly fifty years of preaching, let me humbly review my convictions. The themes must have infinite relations with God and eternity. I have solicited my sermon topics with reverence and, I trust, dignity. I have endeavored to be logical rather than emotional. I know that we are to do more than instruct—we are to persuade, but with heat. I have called for light. Both sides of the coin must be made known. The tendency is to emphasize our own inclinations and cultural training. The preacher must realize that to be agreeable with the disagreeable in the congregation he must accept criticism, knowing he cannot attain one hundred per cent approval. The successful preacher enters the pulpit with the highest motive and motivation. Prayer and meditation must precede his sermon, but, before a congregation, we note the ostentation and the act detracts and takes away reverence. He is not there to give entertainment nor to win applause nor to discharge a professional task. The end is not in self but in ministering to the culture of the souls of the people—to the spirit and immortal nature of man. The congregation is there to partake of the divine life. The end is to free, exalt, sanctify, and perfect the whole personality.

The paramount issues can be expressed, I believe, in three words: man—duty—God. The preacher is necessarily a psychologist, for he knows the nature, condition, and destiny of the soul. The highest privilege in this world is to help save a soul from ruin, to redeem it from thraldom, to bring it to God, to prepare it for immortality. Anything short of this is to make the ministry a caricature. This is the work of the sacred office. The minister is ordained for this purpose.

The instrument to effect this result is *truth,* i. e., *Christian truth.* Preach Christ, not philosophy, nor maxims of conventional morality, nor the folly of human wisdom and the tendency toward pageantry. Preach the Word! Preach Christ, the Son of God, the Savior of men, Christ crucified yet risen, Christ the sufferer, but the Master—Christ the image of God and the model for man. The New Testament is the text book, not merely to get a text (which is often my weakness), but to draw thence the doctrine and persuasion— Jesus, the study and source of inspiration. Utter the truth, be it popular or unpopular; let it strike where it will, we must be honest! The end of preaching is not to communicate exclusively new views but also to awaken attention to old ones, not to feed the mind but to quicken it; not to educate the intellect so much as to direct the conscience and soften and elevate the heart. The end of preaching is effect! Let us not fear the psychology back of this term. The commission is more than instruction, it is for persuasion. Preaching should aim at effect and the best preaching is effectual preaching. If a man rises in the pulpit to read or recite a beautiful piece of composition which sends away the hearers with their praise of his scholarship and his eloquence, but with their hearts bare of impression, this is not preaching. It may be beautiful, it may be eloquent, it may be very good in the classroom or hall—it is not preaching. He preaches who makes people feel and act, who leads them to examine themselves and to live as Christians should live. Moral impression and spiritual life are the criteria of good preaching. This can only come from the soul. The minister preaches for action.

The power desired can only be channeled by sympathy, brought about by the utterance of the preacher. The state of mind to be awakened must be a religious state—a state of strong interest in Christ and the church. Call this love of souls, zeal, fanaticism, or by whatever name you care to use, it must be in the ambassador of God. This is not the revival emotionalism that comes once a year, but a Sunday to Sunday obligation. Before every preacher there are people burdened with sin, yet heirs of eternal life. He may gain admiration, or loud praise, or be idolized for great talent and cultural gifts. This does not guarantee his administrations "in the fullness of the blessing of the Gospel of Christ," unless he has caught that spirit of devotedness which carried Christ to crucifixion that He "might draw all men unto Himself" and which prompted Paul to "become all things to all men, that I might by all means save some."

It is not a system, but a Savior we preach. It is the fellowship of His heart, the love God mediated through Him, the willing surrender of the soul to all His purposes, which brings that unification of the spirit which is at once its peace and power. Apart from Him we can do nothing.

"Blest is the man who sets his soul's desire
Upon a dream, Though half the world forsake him,
Renown will read his log of faith and fire;
And praise, no more than blame, will never shake him.

He seeks a new way; Tempests will not stay him,
Nor lies, nor threats, nor blows, nor bleak derision;
Nor man's nor nature's malice will dismay him,
Who holds before his eyes a noble vision."

—Auslander

THE ETERNAL REFUGE

Text: "The eternal God is thy refuge, and underneath are
the everlasting arms."

—Deuteronomy 33:27

Moses stands pre-eminent in a solitary and uncontested
greatness. Viewed from whatever angle, he looms upon the
horizon of history as a mighty man. Moses, as a legislator,
gave the world its highest code of laws; as a soldier he shines
with military brilliance brighter than Cyrus, Xerxes, Han-
nibal, Alexander or Caesar; as a scholar and seer, he takes
first rank in all ages; as a poet, he lives amid the undimmed
beauty of his undying poems and psalms. A humanitarian, he
stands beside the world's greatest philanthropists; as a
prophet of God, his message still burns with revolutionary
fire, proclaiming the everlastingness, the greatness of the law
and the Kingdom of God. Moses' works are as applicable to
the twentieth century as to the ancient Jews; as a statesman
and nation builder, he leads the world. He came to the rescue
of his people at a time when the Israelites had been so long
subjected and enslaved that the very sentiment of nationality
had gone down, and the hope of deliverance had died.
Unaided by any powerful personage, mocked by every race
for whom he toiled, Moses succeeded in the most tremendous
and hopeless task ever attempted by man. He fanned the
dying embers until the fire of national hope was rekindled;
collected the scattered units of a crushed people into the
invincible confederacy; achieved their liberty; shaped a mob
into an army; an army into a nation; imbued them with
spirit, vision and glorious ideals. Today, the Jew, after six
thousand years, is still what Moses made him.

Our text is the immortal swan song, when Moses passed
from the companionship of earth to the august presence of

19

God. The words were spoken to his soul before they were uttered to his people. Students of Hebrew literature consider these words the loftiest utterance ever made: "The eternal God is thy refuge, and underneath are the everlasting arms." It was fitting that such a life should end as it did on the heights of Nebo, with God. We confess, we rebel at the death of greatness, but death comes in obedience to the will of God.

> "The boast of heraldry, the pomp of power
> All that life, all that beauty, e'er gave
> Await alike the inevitable hour
> The path of glory leads but to the grave."

This sublime fact obliterates the gloomy doctrine of fatalism. The omniscient Creator of the universe is the loving Father and Divine Arbiter of the eternal destinies of His children. Moses died amid his unfinished work and unrealized ideals. The deliverance of Israel was consummated under another leader. Only with his physical eye did Moses behold the land of Canaan, the promised land. It seems the cruel mockery of fate. Moses still speaks! His law is still the essence and inspiration of all law; his ethics are unsurpassed save only by the Sermon on the Mount; his name is synonymous with all heroic virtues that make life generally worth living.

Before the tender ties of years were to be broken, he gave his parting blessing, a benediction and a counsel. Their joy had been his joy, their sorrow his, their burden his, and their victory was to be his victory. Destiny was now entrusted to them. What could he say that would endure, survive the ravishes of time, and be perennially remembered?—only this: "The eternal God is thy refuge, and underneath are the everlasting arms."

> "O God, our help in ages past,
> Our hope for years to come;
> Our shelter from the stormy blast
> And our eternal home."

We know at the heart of the universe there is intelligence, omnipotence, justice, mercy, truth, and love. We are not unmindful of the skepticism abroad today; many philosophers are homeless beings in a vast, heartless universe. Heinrich Heine, the brilliant German poet of the last century, has a striking lyric in which he calls attention to the "Riddle of the Universe." It is a picture of youth calling to the winds, waves, and stars to solve the riddle of the universe; but the only answer is an echo of his cry. If doubt is honest, and much of it is honest, then let us greet it with a mood akin to reverence. Tennyson, in "In Memoriam," writes, "There is more faith in honest doubt, believe me, than in half the creeds." The Chrisitan doubts, like every thinking man, but he doubts his doubts. Browning says, "With me, faith means perpetual unbelief kept quiet." To say that we cannot know the answers to ultimate questions just because these are difficult, is of course, to settle in favor of agnosticism. No progress can be made if agnosticism is adopted and prolonged. We may doubt this power making for righteousness not our own, but not for long. As beauty seeks the artist, harmony the composer, social idealism the reformer, truth the scientist, and righteousness the moralist—in like manner, God seeks the soul of man. Augustine's words ring true, "The soul of man cannot find peace, until it finds rest in God."

What is there underneath the things we see? There are many answers. From antiquity in mythology and legends, we have the world upheld by the elephant who is held up by the tortoise. This is a Hindu legend. The ancient Greeks had the strong man, Atlas, carrying the weight of the globe. The stories are numberless; but there comes out of the ancient world a sublime concept which is canonized and enshrined in the minds of men, "The eternal God is thy refuge and underneath are the everlasting arms." Arms, Moses knew, symbolized power. Bacon, the father of inductive philosophy, pointed out that infinite mind must be antecedent to all phenomena. No following of sequences can find explanation without having recourse to God. Every cause has an effect and every effect has a cause. Simply expressed, we say that there must be a First Cause, or perhaps a First Principle. Schleiermacher defines it as "the feeling of absolute dependence." Dr. Ames defines my expression of religion, "the consciousness of the greatest values of life." Robert Millikan, the eminent physicist, writes, "When we seek to understand existence, we find a something, a power, a being, to give it meaning." Michael Pupin, the professor of electro-mechanics, writes, "I do not believe there is a God, I know there is a God." Herbert Spencer speaks of "the infinite energy from which all things proceed." We would say, in class, "In the world of law, there must be a Law Giver." George Santayana declared, "The human intellect ought to look both ways–study the world scientifically and live spiritually." In our brief transit across the stage of time, from eternity to eternity, and from God to God, under the inexorable laws of science and the insoluble mysteries of religion, we ought to hear the ultimate–"The eternal God–the everlasting arms."

I hear, "All that has been said centuries ago." Today we have a feverish passion for tinkering with everything that is old. We try all kinds of experiments and tests. I am modern, and, I believe, progressive and liberal, but still I believe there are some things definitely fixed once and for all. They do not need alteration or change, they cannot be improved upon. In all our enthusiasm for progress, and with all our interest in new ideas and new things, we need to remember certain foundations are laid, forever and ever. The fundamental of human character remains. We have overthrown many old moralities for social novelties. The world is in turmoil, and never more corrupt than at this hour. Take a long, hard look at the record. Of course, some morals of yesterday had to change. Today we are excessivley given up to the idea that all things must be made new, and at once. Some of us have immense faith in the worth of certain settled facts. How often we relax our own self-discipline, in order to make our lives softer and easier! We pay the price in weak wills and flabby consciences, and loss of influence.

I feel we need heartening. We need a new hold upon the old way of sound living. In my library, I have twelve volumes that are priceless, written by "J. B.", Jonathan Brierley. The last thing he wrote was: "Believe in the tempest's fiercest hour, that the world you are in, is water tight and is not going to flounder. You are in a world of loose ends and the handling of them calls for every atom of strength and courage that is in you. But the farther ends are not loose; they are gripped by a hand that is both love and omnipotent."

Let us remember, ancient Greece has vanished, but not the songs of Homer; imperial Rome has crumbled, but not the strains of Virgil and Dante; Babylon vanished, but not the hanging gardens; Egypt faded, but not the pyramids; Greece wasted, but not the passion for beauty. Eternal truth is like a city with fixed foundations whose Builder and Maker is God; underneath are the everlasting arms. Read the testimony of history. We have been absorbed in our new visions, the new conceptions, and the changed outlook. I seriously ask if we may not have obscured the old things that have not changed one iota in all the years of time. I wonder if there is not a sense of lack, a consciousness of real hunger, an ache in the heart, for the substantial and eternal truths of an unchangeable spiritual religion. Of course, it is interesting to know the new. It is part of intelligent faith; but the deepest and best things of life are not new; they are old, very old indeed. ask: "Are you satisfied with your religious life? Do you feel down in your honest soul that you are getting either the best or the most of your Christian faith? Is it vital? Is it commanding? Does it determine and decide your behavior and your ideas of life? Do we care very much one way or another about this entire matter of taking sides with Jesus Christ in His fight to win this world to right living and right thinking? Does the church of God seem especially necessary"?

The only answer I have, is the timely, timeless, benediction of .Moses, "The eternal God is thy refuge and underneath are the everlasting arms." Job cried, "O, that I knew where I might find Him." Moses answered the cry, and Christ illustrated it. Christ is the eternal refuge. The universe was behind Him, God within Him, this is the end toward which the whole creation moves. Today we think of the heartaches, the perplexed people, suicides, distraught, mentally disturbed, broken homes, and violence everywhere. From Paul's Mamertine prison in Rome, come the words, "All things work together for good to them that love God." We need rest and peace, security and courage, and the assurance is given us: "God is our refuge"—in sorrow, storm, bereavement—"underneath are the everlasting arms." We are modern but still we hunger and thirst for the living God—the Gospel of a Savior from sin, for righteousness that comes from doing the will of God. This is the way toward the eternal city.

F. L. Hosmer has given us these verses:

"One thought I have, my ample creed,
So deep it is and broad,
And equal to my every need
It is the thought of God.

At night my gladness is my prayer;
I drop the daily load,
And every care is pillowed there
Upon the thought of God.

Be still the light upon my way,
My pilgrim staff and rod,
My rest by night, my strength by day,
A blessed thought of God."

THE CONTEMPORARY CHRIST

Text: "Ye shall see Me."

−John 16:16

This is a bold prophecy to declare that man will have a real, vital companionship with the Christ through the ages. However, this is Christianity, it is Christ projected across the centuries. Not what He did, nor what He said, but what He was—this is personality, eternal in the heavens. To the materialist, this is utterly incredible, yet it is the abiding reality that transcends time and space. It is not what we think about His personality or His claims or the interpretation of His message or what we are taught to say about Him; it is an experience, "Once I was blind, now I see," which argument cannot refute.

We all know Christ was a preacher and teacher of sublime truths, that He lived a marvelous life some nineteen hundred and fifty years ago, and that He was crucified on a cross, and that He was raised from the dead. All of this is included in the Christian faith, but if it is in the past tense, He is only a figure of history. Our Christianity, if it is vital and vitalizing, will repeat, "Not that He arose, but He is Risen!" He declared, "I am with you always, even unto the end of the world."—Matthew 28:20, the last words of Matthew's gospel.

We wonder at His enduring quality for few men in history are remembered after the century. His very language is dead, he spoke the vernacular Aramaic. The history of His period has little significance for the present. The one thing we learn from history is our ability to trace the crucifixions of Christ and the resurrections. The Roman age had self-sufficiency and pride, wealth and power. Roman military might ruled the world. The golden milestone was the forum,

25

the center of that ancient world. All around the Mediter-
ranean basin the nations acknowledged the sovereignty of the
pagan Caesars. There were persecutions, aggression, and an
iron throne; everything but moral values and ethical practices. It was into this world that a peasant carpenter entered.
He came out of obscurity and poverty. He began at thirty
years of age, to preach, heal, and teach. A few gathered about
Him because of the sublimity and purity of His life. His
words and deeds challenged the statesmen, churchmen, and
commercial leaders; and then the Jewish religionists and the
Roman rulers ordered Him crucified.

He was abandoned by everyone save His mother and a
few friends, particularly the women who were the last at the
cross and the first at the tomb. Rome sealed the tomb, He
was dead, that was the end! It was but the beginning! His
timid band of cringing followers came out of hiding and
became heroes. In fact, they dared the Roman monarchs in
their palaces. There is nothing like it in all history. They
declared unequivocally that He walked by their sides, an
unseen Presence, but a real one. It was His power, His faith,
His courage that inspired them. In the arena, they lifted their
eyes toward Him and clasped the cross as the starving lions
attacked. In prison, they sang hymns to glorify His Name.
The Romans marveled and wondered, and many believed.
History bears evidence to all of this.

Before three centuries had passed, the Roman eagle was
replaced by the cross; and the ancient pagan temples became
Christian churches. When the powers of the world could not
conquer Christ, they appropriated Him. Jewish dogmatists,
with their doctrine of sacrifice, then made Him a bloody
victim on the altar—"the Lamb slain from the foundation of
the world." The Romans crowned Him King and gorgeously
robed Him in regal splendor. The vestments became all-
important. The Greeks incorporated their mysteries and
occultism, and they, too, appropriated Him. The three
blended together and we have Christ entombed in the

dogmatism of Judaism, the imperialism of Rome and the ecstasy of Greek mysticism.

The world outreach was growing; the seven seas were coming into history. The world was learning that there were colored races, and man with agricultural genius was turning deserts into gardens. There was growth in knowledge and in art. Libraries were coming into being, and temples were being constructed. In a renaissance the resurrection was beginning. Luther nailed his ninety-five theses on the Wittenberg Church door. The German reformation stripped away most of the newer doctrines which Christ had never mentioned, and this was instrumental in breaking the seal of an infallible church and bringing Christ out of the tomb. It was an inevitable resurrection,—"Ye shall see Me." It was Christ—not an ecclesiastical organization, as perfect as the Roman military.

In our modern world there was another attempt to bury Christ in the growth of fundamentalism and modernism. The church had to bring Christ out of the grave clothes of division. It was the controversy of the religion *about* Christ or the religion *of* Christ. Today the division is again growing and the church, with the social gospel and the personal gosepl, again, is burying the Christ. The exclusive emphases are on the saving of souls by the priest, or on the saving of society by the prophet. Our theme is mandatory and indispensable at this time. We need again to resurrect the Christ—"Ye shall see Me."

This is the only testimony to which the world will listen in this age of criticism, examination and verification. We need to see the Man of Galilee, made perfect through suffering. Christ is the great contemporary. We have seen Him walk in Labrador when Grenfell declared Christ walked with Him through the shoals and reefs of that frozen land. He walked with Stanley Jones in India, it was "the Christ of the Indian Road." This is the story of Christ in life: in the deserts of Africa with Augustine, in Umbria with Francis of Assisi, with

Savonarola in Florence, with Bunyan in the Bedford jail.
Regardless of time and place—"I am with you unto the end
of the world." This declaration is like the flow of the river, it
never ceases. I have often quoted Zinzendorf: "I have but
One passion—it is He! even He!" Men like Sadhu Sunder
Singh, Mahatma Gandhi, Schweitzer and many others have
lived with the Son of God and have banished prejudice,
enlightened our understanding, and corrected many of our
mistakes. Listen to Kagawa, as I heard him a number of
times: "There is one body, and one spirit; even as ye are
called to one hope of your calling, one Lord, one faith, one
baptism, one God and Father of all, Who is over all and
through all and in all."

There are thousands who know that Christ is the Great
Contemporary; they have experienced Him in joy and
sorrow, in season and out of season; He is a present help in
time of trouble. John Oxenham has written:

"Not what, but Whom, I do believe
That, in my darkest hour of need,
Hath comfort that no mortal creed
To mortal man may give.

Not what but Whom!
For Christ is more than all the creeds,
And His full life of gentle deeds
Shall all the creeds outlive.

Not what I do believe, but Whom!
Who walks beside me in the gloom?
Who shares the burden wearisome?
Who all the dim way doth illume,
And bids me look beyond the tomb
The larger life to live?

Not what I do believe, but Whom!
Not what but Whom!

How can we know His living Presence? How do we know
He is the contemporary and abiding Christ, the same

yesterday, today and forever? I believe we know in spite of our critical and materialistic age. There are many sophisticated and counterfeit persons living among us, nevertheless we are haunted by His Presence. In spite of all the cynical comments about the church, there is little flippant talk when the Christ is under judgment. We want to make His life real in our own. The way is the way of all truth—"Except ye become as a child." This is not childishness but childlikeness. It is the way of all science, yet some believe science is contrary to Christianity. In practice, no one is more curious, humble and simple than the scientist. He knows that he does not know. Every day he learns; and he knows less and less about more and more. He looks out to this great mysterious world and the vast universe offers the challenge of omnipotence.

There are three steps the scientist will take: 1. Hypothesis; 2. Experiment; 3. Conviction. First, he says that certain facts imply certain truths. On this basis, he experiments with the facts and then determines what is true and what is false. At last comes conviction of the truth.

In this simple, direct way, every one of us may test the real presence of Christ. We can test whether He spoke the truth. We first have to assume the Christ of the Gospel is a Living Presence—then we experiment. We submit every act and word to the test of His Spirit and ask whether our thoughts and our words and our deeds are what He would have us think, say and do. It is a challenge and a searching experiment that will call for every atom of courage we can muster. It is so much easier to live our lives without Him. Life does not make such strong demands. We can keep our ideas and acts on a pretty low level;—but walk with Him, talk with Him, as they did on the road to Emmaus, listen to His counsel, and life becomes difficult. We have to take up a cross; we soon find He is the most alive personality in all of life—"I am the way, the truth and the life."

We will not find Him by argument. He is not a doctrine; He is not dogma; He is not litany, ritual or ceremony. He is not theology nor creed, we find Christ only by living with Him. The great failure and defect of the church through the ages, has been and is today, that we preach a religion about Christ, but do not live the religion of Christ. Let us examine ourselves and not the church. Is He with us? Do we know He is with us? Are we sure we are on His side and by His side? Is it all a dream, a hope, a belief?

CHRISTIAN REALISM FOR THIS AGE

Text: "He considered me trustworthy and appointed me to
the ministry."
—I Timothy 1:12

I greatly appreciate this privilege granted me by the
Presbytery. I realize this opportunity is given me because of
my relationship to the candidate for ordination. We adhere in
this Assembly to the ancient custom of offering advice to the
novitiate who passes from the school of theory to the school
of practice.

This ecclesiastical observance goes back to the practice in
Old Testament times when Eli commissioned Samuel and
annointed him. Our textual content reminds us of the
veteran, Paul, challenging young Timothy. This apostolic
benediction and the laying on of the hands of presbyters
moves me emotionally, perhaps beyond my powers of
expression. There will be tonight rigorous imperatives given
him to bring my son into the teaching eldership of the
church.

I am fully aware that the seminary has not made a saint
out of him. I am too much of a prelapsarian Presbyterian and
a believer in Calvinistic depravity, to think the ordination
ritual will exorcise from him the inherent tendency of the
low born urge. Back of this dedication is a seminary training,
and back of the seminary are college and high school, and
back of the school are childhood and infancy, and back of all
this are a praying father and mother asking God to consecrate
him to Christ and the Church. My prayer now is written in
the Lord's earliest recorded words, "Wist ye not that I must
be about my Father's business?" William Blake, the mystic,
has a paragraph which expresses my desire. He writes:

31

"O my son, my son, I know little the path thou goest
But lo! there is a God Who made heaven and earth;
Stretch out thy hand to Him."

Paul begins with Timothy: "I thank Jesus Christ Who
made this possible. He considered me trustworthy and
appointed me to the ministry." This is the doctrine of
election, not elected by society nor by an ecclesiastical ruler,
but elected by our Father Which art in Heaven. The minister
of Jesus Christ is to discern "a light never seen on sea or
land." He is to hear a voice above the cannon, the steam
shovel and the stock exchange. The things needful in
Christian realism are humility and exultation. The humility is
human dependency, the exultation is Divine supremacy.
When the minister reflects upon the infinite, he naturally
formulates a concept of himself and the universe and the
Author of both. It is then he reverently cries, "Thine is the
kingdom, the power, and the glory, forever and ever."

As an ambassador of God, he then becomes a light in a
dark world, a voice of pity in a hard world, a rebuker of
injustice in a warring world, a pleader of virtue in a vulgar
world, and a witness for Christ throughout the world. His is a
throne of beauty, a citadel of integrity, a watch tower of
hope. The real minister has the soul of a mystic and the
ethical interest of a prophet. His office is sacramental,
therefore it is creative and dynamic unto salvation. It belongs
to him not only because of tradition, temperament, eloquence, poetic gift, or social passion; but first and foremost
because he belongs to the Most High.

This brings me to the first thing I would like to say. For
a genuine service to our Lord and Master, the first requirement is naturally the first commandment, *"Love God."*
This is paramount and indispensable to the minister. It is his
motivation. To him, the unseen is more than the seen; the
unknown will encompass the known; the walk by faith will
be infinitely more than the walk by sight; the higher he

aspires the farther the ideal will recede; and the truer he becomes, the more commanding will be his sense of right.

"God's greatness
Flows around our incompleteness.
'Round our restlessness, His rest."

Dr. Whitehead, perhaps the finest, religious, philosophic mind of this century, writes: "Religion is the vision of something which stands beyond, behind, and within the passing flux of immediate things—something which is real and yet waiting to be realized—something which is remotely possible and yet the greatest of all possible facts—something that gives meaning to all that passes, yet it eludes our comprehension." We immediately see that this definition is something more than moral earnestness, eager intellectualism, or theology. It is more than a debatable issue—it is a declaration! It is what Einstein called the "cosmic sense."

The preacher preaches the ideal of the Master Who said, "Be perfect even as your Father in Heaven is perfect." This is Christian realism at its highest and best. In its final analysis, Christianity does not rest on argument but on personal experience. The minister cannot give something he does not possess. He must reveal God as God has been revealed to him. He is to tap spiritual resources. He is to meditate upon eternal verities. He is to follow the injunction of the Scriptures, "Worship the Father in spirit and in truth, for the Father seeketh such to worship him." This is the minister's clear call to prayer, meditation, communion, fellowship with the spirit, and a closer walk with the living God. He is not interested in definitions. Correctly phrased orthodoxy or carefully phrased liberalism will not meet his requirement. He must have Christian realism that sees all issues in the light of eternity. To use the colloquialism, he is not part of the passing show; he is a judge of the passing show. He sets the things of time against the background of eternity. The order of progress is now, and ever has been, "a new heaven," then, "a new earth, wherein dwelleth righteousness."

Strange indeed, that a minister of Jesus Christ should look to scientific men, modern philosophers, contemporary economists, or pseudo-psychiatrists for the last word. Religion is never to be brought down to the level of reason. The minister's religion is an art and not a science. There is no changing point of view; he does not prophesy mutabilities. Contemporary religion is a contradiction of terms. Religion is not at the mercy of a passing critic. It is not subject to the logical syllogisms of the logician or philosopher. Philosophic thinking, however, will be of use in explicating what is implicated in religious experience. George Bernard Shaw gazed at the Grand Canyon in Arizona and the Irish dramatist, after long silence, said: "This reminds me of religion. Science changes every twenty years and we change our minds continually. Religion is like the canyon—it is always the same."

The second requirement is like unto it: *"Love thy neighbor."* Love God—love men. We cannot forget that all the moral and humanitarian teachings of the Christ were religiously motivated. He does not ask what is sociologically sound, but rather what is religiously acceptable. Jesus was always more concerned with the doer of the good than with the recipient of the good, with the helper rather than with the one helped. Many go so far as to say that He was a second Moses and that Christianity is simply the revised law, or that crystallized Christianity is morality.

If we again turn to the days of the prophets, we recall that they scorned social injustice, unfair practices, and dishonest weights and measures. Amos shouted: "God hates your sacrifices and your worship. Let justice roll down like water and righteousness like the waves of the sea." Isaiah pictures God at the door of the temple, crying: "Why trample my courts? Do justice, release the oppressed." James, the brother of our Lord, declared: "Pure religion and undefiled before God is to visit the fatherless, the widows in affliction and to keep oneself unspotted from the world."

Humanists could not define religion more effectively than this.

The Christian minister teaches: "Ye must be the salt of the earth,"—in other words, the saving power of human society; "Ye are the light of the world," the illuminating power of society; "Ye are the leaven," the transforming power of society. Christ always unites spiritual experience with social service, the unseen with the seen, the ideal with the factual, the eternal with the temporal. In harmony both are right; in over-emphasis both are wrong. Religion is basically balance, poise, compensation. Mysticism and realism are not incompatible.

The inner life without outward service is thin and poor. The outward life without the spirit is dull and heavy. The spirit without the body is impotent but the body without the spirit is dead. Christianity must justify its claims not merely by what it says but by what it does, not only by creeds but by deeds, not only by saving men, but by saving society. Briefly, I would say it must become suffused by humanitarian ethics filled with the fraternal spirit. It is a *saved soul* in a *saved body* living in a *saved community*.

The Christian minister is, in reality, the practical man of affairs. The sons of Mary must lead the sons of Martha. It was the prophet, seeing the Lord high and lifted up, who was the real reformer and statesman. Plato, the God-intoxicated philosopher, was the real advocate of the Republic. The divine dreamer, Augustine, was the real servant of the people and the church. The fugitive earthly scene is permeated with the eternal. In the storm of life the compass invariably points to the north pole. The minister of the Gospel must realize that his ethical ideals grow out of moral insight. Religion must be shared to be kept. A faith that is not contagious is not vital. Religion does more than instruct, it infects. It is not only taught, it is caught. An impersonal religion is impossible. The problem confronting the prophet is in reality not an economic one nor is it a political one nor a social one. It is fundamentally a problem of the heart. "Out of the heart flow the issues of life." Without a God-like character, the most perfect system will fail. *A consecrated personal life is the primary task of the minister.* Christ made it clear that existence is physical and dependent upon the energy of matter. Life is spiritual and dependent upon the energy of the soul. The first social and moral duty of the pastor is to create soul energy in man and thus transform existence into life—yea, even life everlasting.

The third requirement naturally follows: *"Love God and man with all your mind."* This calls for intellectual respectability. The minister must keep abreast of current events and experimental research. He realizes, however, that the best knowledge of the day is not religion; timely information is not the wisdom of eternity; spiritual reality is more than new concepts and associations. The church is not his platform nor ethical center; it is redemptive in its mission and commission. The church under his leadership may be full of energy but anemic in soul. It may be a rummage sale center with a static faith. It is easy to do Christian work; it is difficult to pray. The Christian scholar is to give the church new ideas, but primarily he is to give it a new birth.

I believe, nevertheless, that education is indispensable to the church and to the minister. The soul of education is the education of the soul. The minister is preparing men to grow out of spiritual ignorance into well rounded maturity. He blends knowledge with character, and facts with moral values. Thomas Arnold expressed it: "teaching our understanding to know the highest truth; teaching our affections to love the highest good." The highest knowledge, after all, is to know good from evil. Christian realism never excommunicates reason. It is never unmindful of psychological drives. The Christian scholar is aware of liquid standards and crumbling authorities. He knows the education of facts has outstripped the education of faith, that the world has taught us how to destroy—now we must teach the world how to construct. We have learned in our scientific laboratories how to take life apart; now, we must show the world how to put life together. We have made life mechanical ; now, we must make it creative. We have developed the technique of collecting facts; now, we must tell the world what to do with them. We have been keen on analysis; now, we must have the ability to interpret. We know the price of things, but let us tell the world values. The technological world has given us the know-how; now we must give that world the know-why. We have been told what the world is made of; now, let us tell the world what it is made for. We have nuclear fission; let us give the world moral accountability. The world has power; let us give it light. The world has speed; let us give it direction. The world has things; let us give it principles.

No religion can long endure unless it rests on these thoroughgoing intellectual foundations. Men will listen to reason and will not sacrifice it for a blind faith. Ignorance is not now, and never has been, the mother of rational devotion. The minister's theology undergoes many trans-formations: science strikes down his mythical theories; criticism pierces many of his traditions; logic is fatal to many of his ecclesiastical dogmas. Let us never forget that regardless of these factors, the more we know, the more we wonder. Man is constitutionally on God's side. He cannot amend the constitution, but he can impair it. He is subject to its laws and is not a legislator. All change is not progress. The stairs which go up also come down. The law of evolution precludes the law of devolution. Men let go of error; they also, at times, let go of truth.

In conclusion, let me say to my little boy who has reached his maturity, that I plead with him and with all of us to *remember the fundamentals.* In this world where eve-rything changes but change, there are certain cardinal principles that remain unshaken. For example, the customs, habits, and gadgets have greatly changed since Shakespeare's day; but Hamlet's indecision, and Lady Macbeth's wrestling, and Portia's pleading for mercy, are from everlasting to everlasting. "The eternal God is thy refuge and underneath are the everlasting arms."

On the football field there is movement, confusion, competition, and a tangled mass of players; but everything associated with the game is not in motion. The goal posts, the rules of the game, and the referees remain the same. The minister of Jesus Christ knows the perennial goal posts we call Truth—Purpose—Morals—Destiny. "A mighty fortress is our God, a bulwark never failing."

I have pleaded tonight for *God's Sovereignty, moral and social values and intellectual respectability,* and I beg of you, translate them and incarnate them into the fullness of the stature of Christ. Yet, we may believe all these things, and fail unless we develop soul power. We may have the finest brushes, paints, canvasses, and subject matter in all the world, and fail because we lack the soul of an artist. The soul that is developed into the likeness of Jesus Christ "loves folks"— loves them for what they are, but more especially for what they may become.

Carlyle cried, "What this parish needs before anything else is a preacher who knows God otherwise than by hear-say."

We commission then, a young man to preach, not an old Gospel—not a new Gospel—but an ageless, timeless, dateless, eternal Gospel of redemption. He should not fiddle upon the trifling tunes of this world and let the city of the soul burn.

> "For each age is a dream that is dying
> Or one that is coming to birth."

This is the ministry for this age: preaching the living words of God to living men.

A MESSAGE FROM JERUSALEM TO ATHENS

Text: "Men of Athens, I perceive that in every way you are
very religious."

—Acts 17:22

Mr. Moderator, members of the Presbytery, and
members and friends of this church: Your mission tonight is
an important one. You are inducting a young man into the
pastorate of this church which is one of the influential
churches of your Presbytery. I deem my part of the program
a personal privilege, and I feel the responsibility very keenly.
I have been with the pastor-elect at his ordination, presided
at the marriage altar, and now share in this form and order of
installation.

The atmosphere tonight is somewhat different from my
own first installation a good many years ago. At that time
there were theological arguments between so-called funda-
mentalists and modernists. Men hated one another for the
love of God. However, the battle of ideas is always vital, and
essentially far-reaching in its influence.

Tonight, the ecclesiastical cross currents are not in the
realm of theology but in sociology. In a large measure the
facts are curiously contradictory. We are in a quandary with a
religious upturn and an ethical downturn. This is an age of
faith and an age of corruption. When the present church
membership is an index of achievement, it is "progress," and
when present social conditions are the criterion, it must be
pronounced "retrogression." The church gains are entirely
statistical, for ethically we are progressively retrogressive.

An ostrich once died in the British Museum Zoo. An
autopsy was ordered to determine the cause; and they found
golf balls, spoons, nails, coins, etc. The examiner's only

comment was, "Lack of protein would kill any of us." The lack of spiritual nourishment will kill the soul-life as it is reflected in the social life today.

The Apostle from Jerusalem had come to Athens; and, to their city of philosophers, poets, historians, and orators, he brought a message of spiritual protein. He had come from the land of prophets where Isaiah, Jeremiah, Ezekiel, Amos, and Hosea had preached social righteousness; the Christ had brought good news of salvation. The prophets had preached duty, the Christ had preached the Kingdom. This was a new religion to the philosophers of Athens.

In this land of Plato, Socrates, Aristotle and Pythagoras, Paul was taken to Mars Hill. On the steps of the Senate, he made Christian morality paramount, but still kept it intellectually respectable. Long before the philosophy of Sir William Hamilton, Paul knew that the greatest thing in life is man, but he rejected the thought that the greatest thing in man is mind. This philosophic evangelist knew that to lose faith in the mind is to lose faith in God who made the mind, yet Paul knew that history is full of brilliant minds with black hearts. "Out of the heart flow the issues of life." This, then, is the greatest thing in man. Pascal was not the first to say, "The heart has reasons which the mind knows not." The bread from Jerusalem had to feed the cultural city starving from a lack of ethical protein and a lack of spiritual waters flowing unto eternal life.

Paul began, "I perceive that in every way you are very religious." Today we would say this is flattery, but excellent homiletics and perfect strategy. Complimenting them, he gained their attention. Paul went on, "I found an altar 'to an unknown God'." Put Paul on the steps of the United States Senate and he could say: "I perceive, Americans, that in every way you are very religious. I read the Saturday paper with hundreds of church notices. I see, many times, two or three churches in a single block. I could go up these Senate steps to a Prayer Room, or turn on the television and see the President and his cabinet come out of that room to conduct the nation's business. I visit the book stores and observe that the best sellers are religious books; in fact, I hear that millions of copies of modern translations of the Bible have been sold in a few months. Passing a lunch counter, I hear the 'juice-box' play 'Faith, Hope and Charity,' 'The Man Upstairs,' and a dozen other jazz hymns. The Sunday morning Drive-In has golfers in sport clothes, singing hymns. All your denominations are in new building campaigns; your ball parks attract thousands to listen to traveling evangelists; your Pledge of Allegiance reads, 'this nation, under God,' and your stamps are sometimes cancelled, reading, 'Pray for peace.' In 1870, only eighteen per cent of the American people belonged to a church or synagogue; now, more than sixty per cent of the people are church members and 35,500,000 children are registered in Sunday School. Americans, you are very religious."

In Athens, he said, "You have many idols and images." "Americans, I see you worship productivity, power, riches, influence, motivation and technology. You are efficiency experts; but remember what Huxley, the scientist, told you: 'Clever men are as common as blackberries, but the rare thing is to find a good one.' The paradox is apparent. The power of good and the power of evil are growing up together."

The Athenians had ignorance in their wisdom; bondage in their freedom; tradition in their progressiveness, or, as Fred Knowles expressed it, "frail strength, weak austerity, and discordant harmony." Paul, in substance, asked, "What about the harvest?" The age that produced atomic energy also produced polluted minds like Hitler and Stalin. Our age of church extension with numerical strength is a period with penal institutions over-crowded and inadequate. Burglary and larceny have increased enormously in the last few years. Narcotics, tax frauds, drunkenness, kidnappers, have multiplied four times faster than the population. The Kinsey report was read with curious interest but with moral indifference. "The times are out of joint."

"You are very religious, but a High School teacher has to resign to drive a beer truck to make a livelihood for his family; a boxing bout lasting ten to fifteen minutes will pay more for fisticuffs than we pay one hundred teachers for an entire month; in an art exhibit, the picture which won first prize was found to have been hung wrong side up. I perceive, Americans, you are like the Athenians. You have doctrines, disciplines, creeds, sacraments, rituals, feasts, fasts, prayers, phylacteries, processionals, recessionals, incense, holy water, confessionals, last unction, and scores of other liturgical observances; but you have lost the Shepherd of the sheep and the Gospel of redemption. You have full churches, with empty souls," says Paul. Goldsmith expressed it:

"Ill fares the land, to hastening ills a prey
Where wealth accumulates, and men decay."

Personally, I love ritual, and I feel that when we get rid of the forms we run the risk of getting rid of the insight. Traditional litany is not against reason but above it. There is a mystical element that transcends the capacity of the mind. Paul said, "Eye hath not seen, nor ear heard, neither hath it entered into the heart of man, what things God hath prepared for them that love Him" (I Corinthinas 2:9). I believe our mission is to re-examine the methods, but to keep the Pauline spirit active and responsive. We have murdered men for doubting the virgin birth and verbal inspiration of Scriptures, but never have we lifted a voice against robbing the poor or enslaving children. We have religion but not Christianity, forms but little devotion.

Isaiah condemned burnt incense, blood offering, sacred feasts, holy days, and many prayers. He said, "When ye spread forth your hands, I will hide mine eyes from you; yea, when ye make many prayers, I will not hear; your hands are full of blood; . . . Put away the evil of your doings . . . seek judgment, relieve the oppressed, judge the fatherless, plead for the widow" (Isaiah 1:15-17). Amos, the shepherd of Tekoa, said: "I hate, I despise your feast days. Let judgment roll down as waters, and righteousness as a mighty stream" (Amos 5:21-24). Micah said: "What doth the Lord require of thee but to do justly, and to love mercy, and to walk humbly with thy God?" (Micah 6:8). The prophets believed that salvation must be understood in terms of morality.

The Athenians did not understand that the "sons of Mary" had "chosen the better part." Paul contended they had symbols but not life, proverbs but not practice, holy days but not a holy life. The Gospel from Galilee had comfort for those who mourned and could give beauty for ashes and the oil of joy to the sorrowful. Athens and America need the pastoral prayers which descend to the depths and rise to the heights. The prophet must come down from the "snows of Lebanon" where he has received purity, light, vision, to feed the valley below. The Jerusalem prophet, with his inner light and insight, brought the principles of character to the men of Athens.

The present need is apparent when we see people flock to the teachers of mysticism, occultism and metaphysics. The quest is everywhere apparent. To ignore or ridicule, to smile or scowl is sheer folly. This vogue is a symptom of something. There is a spiritual and emotional hunger, and the Christian Gospel must meet it. We must make religious attendance a spiritual experience. Milton said, "When I go to church, I want to hear about God." The people must hear the voice from behind the hills and visualize the angels of God ascending and descending. We have minimized the mystical and left people hungry. Men must be brought to the realization that they are creatures of eternity now living in time. I do not believe that the ritual of the Sadducees or the ecclesiastical codes of the Pharisees will suffice. There must be a mystical interpretation of our Christianity. If the forms in the church are not vital, throw them out; if they are too idealistic, put them to work; if they are exclusively of the emotions, harness them to the will; if they are abstract, make them concrete; if they are too theoretical, make them practical; if they are hypotheses, bring them to a conclusion; and if they are beautiful in a dream-world, make them beautiful in the world of realism. Let us get religion out of meaningless niceties and baffling metaphysics, and bring it into the work-a-day world of practical realism. We must be effective and make personal evangelism part of our social gospel. Moral progress is contingent upon moral power. The world must have the priest's uplift and the prophet's righteousness. We must bring the Jerusalem righteousness to the mystical urge in Athens.

In the end, it is not sociology we need, but redemption; it is not progress, but pardon; it is not renovation, but regeneration; it is not survival, but revival; not abundant life, but the eternal life. When the church succeeds in these spiritual elements, the church will become the monitor of the race and the molder of its destiny. Paul told Timothy to guard against keeping the forms of religion and neglecting its force. We must never mistake quantity for quality, nor numbers for strength, nor external appearance for internal worth. America is very religious, but is not always ʿhristlike. Athens had cold statues, not warm hearts. Ameiʿa, like Athens, must learn that she can become spiritually mangled in the wheels of social machinery.

Tonight, you install a young man with energy, courage, initiative, ambition, and enthusiasm. I beg of him never to obscure the fundamentals or becloud issues. The apostleship is the same yesterday, and today, and will be forever. This is equally true of prophecy. The whole mission and commission remains, "Follow thou Me." Christ calls it the holy way of life. Holiness is wholesomeness; it is wholeness and it is "seeing life through and seeing it whole."

I wish I were back at my first installation. Knowing the trials, the tribulations, I would still accept my vows and pledge anew my service to make Christ Lord of all. I cannot say more to my son than General Smuts of South Africa said: "It is a poor tribute to our fathers to camp where they fell." The Gospel he preaches must be a great indicative and not merely a great imperative. His greatest mandate will be his love of Jesus Christ, his faith in God, his devotion to the Kingdom, and his loyalty to the church. He has one goal: to see men, women, and children "born again," and I speak in the deepest sense of the New Testament meaning, to be "born from above." I repeat, we may be very religious but un-Christian. We can say these things from the altar of the Living God and from the Senate steps in Washington and from the courthouse steps of any county in America.

This is not a new Gospel I have given, but the endless old Gospel, giving us new life for the individual and for society. My only mission is to restate the rich content of our Christian faith. The minister's mission in the church is to have a flaming message of conviction which gladdens and inspires. It must have in it "the power of an endless life."

I would like to close with a personal message to your pastor-elect from his mother's pen, adapted from verses by Ralph S. Centiman.

> "I do not ask
> That crowds may throng the temple—
> Pale honor, that, which leaves a fading glow—
> I only ask that as he speaks the message
> His Christ, the souls who hear,
> May see and know.

> I do not ask
> For churchly pomp or pageant
> For choirs and music wealth alone can build—
> I only ask that he may speak the message
> To hearts, which, empty, finding
> God, are filled.

I do not ask
For earthly place or laurel—
Distinction that is crowned in shining sun—
I only ask that when he speaks the message
The Father's peace may come,
His will be done."

OUR FATHER

Text: "Our Father, Which art in Heaven."

—Luke 11:2

It has been said that Christianity is simply a natural growth from pre-existing philosophy; it is built upon a theistic concept; it is a belief in someone or something called God. I believe this is a mistake historically and philosophically. There is nothing in all philosophy or literature that implies a divine father, a personal God, Who stands in helpful relations to men, guiding, consoling, and comforting them. There has been deism, which is a general belief in a superior power. There has been a hypothesis that back of all phenomena there is a certain divine wisdom. There has never been a concept of real filial relation with the Divine such as father and child. This is unknown outside Christianity.

Among the oldest religions of the world, such as Brahmanism in India, or, in its later form, Buddhism, there is no concept of fatherhood. There is, at the most, a belief in a great inscrutable, unknowable power, never defined and never analyzed. It is difficult to love or trust or truly worship a god who does not feel, or a god who does not love. A god without thought or knowledge or love is certainly not a father. This can be said of world religions in general.

The old religions of Greece and Rome are devoid of any kind of reference to the fatherhood of god. You will find among the poets who reflect the common sentiment of the common people, humanized gods—gods dragged down to the likeness of men, or deified men, men raised to the stature of gods. You will find among the philosophers—Marcus Aurelius, Seneca, the stoics, belief in a god; but a god that is forever unknown. The altar which Paul saw in Athens expressed itself in two words, the very best in pagan

47

literature. There is infinite pathos in it, "Ye men of Athens, in all things I perceive you are very religious. I found an altar with this inscription, 'To an Unknown God', (Agnosto Theo)." This is paganism's best expression of faith; the world has been orphaned. The orphaned world has had a sense that there is somewhere a father; and it has been looking, often through tears, looking, "if haply they might find Him." There has *never* been faith, love, or confidence in a Divine Father.

Some Bible students may ask, "Was there not a fatherhood of God in the Old Testament? Did not David say 'like as a father pitieth his children'? Did not Isaiah say, 'Thou art our Father, though we are ignorant of Thee'?" Yes, there is the teaching of fatherhood in the Old Testament. There is no separation between the Gospel and the law and the prophets. Jesus is the end of law, the fulfillment of the law. "Think not that I came to destroy the law or the prophets, I came not to destroy, but to fulfill." The Gospel began in the first chapter of Genesis, in the teaching that God created man in His own image, the seed from which the whole Gospel sprang. God is our Father and we are His children; we are made in His likeness. There is a kinship between God and man; this kinship enables God to talk with men, and enables men to be followers with Him. This truth grows clearer and more clear as we review book after book, until it comes into full blossom in the teaching of God dwelling in human flesh, manifesting Himself through the perfect experience. The revelation shows a sinless life in order that the divine and the sinless human life might henceforth go hand in hand—more than that, that the divine and the human might be indissolubly united, brought together in one, and go together through eternity. The distinctively Christian conception of God is, that He is "the Father of our spirits" (Hebrews 12:9). The fatherhood in the Old Testament emphasizes the attributes of aloofness and sovereignty. We know the content of the fatherly element in the Old Testament refers to the father of a chosen nation, "them that fear Him" (Psalm 103:13). Never once does the Old Testament intimate that Jehovah is the *universal father* of all mankind. He is incomprehensibly arbitrary. Jesus' characteristic designation for God is reported one hundred and fifty times in the four Gospels, to be, "Father," used in various connections. This is the basic fact of Christ's mission, to reveal the Father. "He that hath seen Me hath seen the Father."

I have intentionally omitted the theological terms and concepts. There are five generic ideas or modes of regarding the Infinite. There is in the Bible, first, the *Creative.* "In the beginning God created." Secondly, we have the *Monarchical,* God as sovereign; thirdly, we have the *Judicial,* God as judge. Fourthly, the *Redemptive,* God as Savior; and the last, which is our concern at this time, the *Paternal,* God as Father. For a complete Biblical review we would have to weld together these five representations for a comprehensive analysis. Let us simply state the catechism and let it temporarily rest there: "God is spirit, infinite, eternal and unchangeable in His being, wisdom, power, holiness, justice, goodness and truth."

Like all preachers of the Gospel, I have been asked countless times: "If God is a Father, righteous, with all power and all justice, why don't we have a righteous society? If the Father hates evil and loves purity, why are the evil not punished and the good not rewarded? There is Viet Nam—an all-powerful God would stop it. An all-good God would prevent all evil; an all-just God would bring justice. If God is good, He is not powerful; if He is powerful, He is not good." There are many cults giving answer to the paradox. One group says, "The outer world is an illusion, a passing dream." Then we are told, "All discord is harmony misunderstood, and all so-called evil is good in the making." One group blindly declares, "Whatever is, is right."

I know that the good often fails and evil often wins. It is not helpful to me to hear that it is a mystery of human life unsolvable. I listen to testimonies that God can heal diseases, but apparently is unable to give a child arms who has been born without them. I ask, "If I pray 'Our Father Which Art in Heaven,' am I thinking of a Father with reason, justice, truth, love?"

First, look at the outward world of atoms and molecules, as enveloped in the law of evolution. We cannot move one atom that does not reverberate throughout the universe. Forces cannot move by chance or whim. The railroad is managed by engineers, signal switches, electrical impulses, and operators along the entire road. There must be order, control, to avoid a wreck. In our universe with combinations of forces so stupendous and so intricate, there must be law obeying the rules of nature with unswerving obedience, without change or deviation.

The same law must prevail in the moral and spiritual universe. Man is a child of God and is able to adjust to environment, not to change the law but to change his methods. He is a free moral agent. He has the power of choice in a universe of law. A father says to his son, "You cannot do good unless you have the choice of good and evil." God, Himself, cannot do everything; He cannot erase yesterday; He cannot build character without the making of a choice. A machine is not moral or immoral. Man is free to bring light out of darkness, truth out of error, success out of failure, strength out of weakness and life out of death.

Law and freedom are not irreconcilable terms. I know a place where men do not drink or steal; they keep regular hours; eat the same meals; attend church Sunday morning— they are in the penitentiary. In the city, men drink to excess, quarrel, are lazy and disorderly, and many do not go to church. In the penitentiary they have law without freedom and in the city they have freedom with law. Which is the better method?

Let me emphasize, the sin is rebuked and the sinner

never escapes. We are not punished *for* our sins but *by* our sins. It may not happen on the outside, but inevitably it has reaction on the inside. Punishment may not come *to* a man but it always comes *in* a man. He may not lose his reputation, but he will lose his character. He may not lose his civil standing, but he will lose his self-respect. He will lose the essentials of life and they include spirituality, fine perception, sensitive conscience and ability to enjoy the good and the best in life.

If God is a Father, then why all the injustice? Perhaps if we could see the whole picture, our judgment would change. Did Epictetus lose as a slave, or Dante as an exile, or Milton in blindness, or Bunyan in jail? We could add hundreds of martyrs, physically deformed, poverty stricken, and the so-called submerged to the list, but the final criterion is character. What does a father want from his child? Above all else, it is character. He will not say, "I will protect you from all limitations, hardships, and failures; but I want you to be a child of your father with honor and credit to your name and your God."

God, in a sense, moves through men who attempt, in someway, to transform things toward the good, the good being greater harmony, less suffering, and more creativeness. How does the Father function? In Wales there is a mountain known as Cadar Idris, cloaked in mists overlooking the Irish sea. Accessibility to the summit is made by paths carved out by the hooves of sheep. It is known at the top as a haunt of beauty. A legend has grown up declaring if a man spends a night on the summit, he will awaken a bard or a fool. Each of us has been there, by tragedy or a set-back. We know the sense of great loneliness, when we have been lashed by a storm in the soul, and in the mental mist. We, too, awaken a poet or a fool. Without this sense of aloneness we never know how we must readjust to the relations of things about us or to our God, our Father.

Tragedy or sorrow, disappointment or confusion, have taken us alone to our own Mount Cadar Idris. When we climbed that peak we felt lonely and lost. We wondered why this trouble had happened to us, and we asked, "Has life any meaning at all?" We awaken, a bard or a fool. We will either gain insight or lose some more of the meaning to which we clutch so desperately. If we come to the realization that we have weaknesses and faults, selfishness and egoisms—if we know we can do better and that we are intended for something higher and greater—if we come to the sure knowledge that what we may become can have cosmic significance—if we learn to respond anew to the beauty of nature—then we will be able to descend from that summit confident that there is a Father Who works through our higher dreams. In the words of Rhys Williams, "We can walk away from tragedy, wiser, greater, and larger and God is not remote."

Christ, Who served the blind and persecuted, ended on the Cross; and died like a thief and malefactor—yet He prayed, "Father, into Thy hands I commend My spirit."

"Keep Thou my feet, I do not ask to see
The distant scene; one step enough for me."

A SPIRITUAL MANDATE

Text: "And the Lord said unto Moses, 'Speak unto the children of Israel, that they go forward'."
—Exodus 14:15

We are aware that people are more interested in current events taking place in Viet Nam, the Near East, Red China, and among the African republics than in the history of the Hebrews four thousand years ago—a nomad tribe on the plains of Sinai. I think, however, our times would register a greater advance in the things worthwhile if they would face all the facts of God. A superficial study of the history of civilization would show the importance of movements that give direction to the human race. In foothills we can step across what will further down stream be the mighty Mississippi, and we realize that the beginnings are important. In 1976 we will celebrate the two hundredth anniversary of what in reality was the birth of a nation.

Our study shows how the Hebrew beginning nearly ended at its birth. No sooner did the slaves escape from Egyptian bondage than they were about to be scalped. They were about to pay for their liberty with their lives. Behind them were cruel masters, thirsting for their blood. Before them were the waters of the Red Sea, likely to be dyed a deeper red with their own hearts' blood. They bitterly reproached their dauntless leader, Moses, for not letting well enough alone and leaving them in Egypt. At this critical juncture, Moses was given the divine illumination to see that their only salvation was to advance: "Speak to the children of Israel, that they go forward."

This was a direct, vigorous command. Jehovah had grown tired of their appeals for help. Having freedom, now it was time for them to accept responsibility. The only help that is permanent is self-help—helping them to help themselves. It was time now for them to show appreciation. Liberty calls for initiative, effort, and self-direction. Freedom adds to duties. Privileges call for moral obligations. Today, we, too, cry for additional freedom; but we fail to realize that favorable advantages in the status quo call for additional effort and infinitely more discipline. We should not expect outside assistance for inside weaknesses. The children of Israel blamed Moses; we blame our leadership. We fail to understand that we cannot have leadership without followship. The general needs every grade of soldier in the army; from top to bottom there must be responsibility. Like the Israelites, many of us stay in the desert and complain. God says, "Go forward," and we stand.

Civilization is at the sea. Behind is the awful carnage. We, too, sigh for the leeks and onions of Egypt. We want to return to the traditional practices of eating off the land, polluting air and water, following the course of least resistance; because, to go forward has risk, discipline, conformity, and sacrifice. We forget that life is a treadmill, and we must go forward or go under. The secret of balance, as in riding a bicycle, is motion. "He who hesitates is lost." The Chinese mystic, Lao Tsu, said: "Who tiptoes totters, who straddles stumbles, who wabbles wallows." Our motto today is *no standing.* In fact, we find it in front of public buildings, fire hydrants and other restricted areas. The old German proverb is, "If we rest, we rust." When the water stops running it stagnates; if the tree rests, it dies; if the heart stops, we die. God's command is "Go forward, or die."

Pilgrim, in his progress, wanted to stop at Vanity Fair. Here were lights, laughter, play, entertainment, and excitement. To reach the Holy City of God, he had to go forward. The Hebrews wanted to worship luxury, the golden calf. It wasn't discipline they wanted, it was ease; not order, but chaos; not regularity, but freedom; not duty, but privilege. We pray for a modern Moses, but when he defines terms and obligations, we, too, rebel. We read of our prophets and the reception given them: John Wesley, the founder of the Methodist Church, was stoned, jeered, and scorned; Dwight L. Moody, in the slums, had more than vulgarity thrown at him, they also used bricks; William Booth of the Salvation Army, was thrown into the London gutter; Christ was spat upon, given a crown of thorns, and crucified. Call upon men to go forward and the prophets are stoned, then and now! Yet, "Righteousness exalteth a nation and sin is a reproach to any people." The sin of mankind is stagnation.

We are not only commissioned to go forward, but also to keep rank. As in any army, there are many types of individuals, with different interests and varying mental capacities. Think of the differences found in the twelve disciples. Christ did not ask them to be alike but rather to be one. When we go forward we cannot all do the same thing in the same way. We are temperamentally different and with different aptitudes, but still we can keep rank and go forward with the same motives. The army cannot be divided and win; internal strife is death. No war is more disastrous than civil war. A divided church cannot make answer to a divided world.

The differences in churches regarding creeds, polity, and ecclesiastical machinery, have killed zeal and reduced the Christian influence. It has gone forward when it has kept the message, spirit and love of Christ. We have to have more than creeds, we must have deeds; we have to have more than words, we have to have action; we have to have more than platitudes, we have to go forward. To do this, we need the truth of the prophets, the zeal of the disciples, and the love of the missionary.

In the church we have members who will give bread and contribute money, but fail to share their faith. Jesus preached in the synagogue and on the mountain side; but, let

us never forget, it was his followers who carried the Gospel to
Europe and Asia, and to the ends of the earth. The Christian
message is, "Go thou, and do likewise." Retreat is unthinkable, surrender is cowardly, and to capitulate is inex-
cusable. Christians are to preach the whole Gospel to the
whole world. To succeed and go forward we need unity of
spirit, enthusiasm, and a high morale. There is no standing
room in the church of Christ; it is a procession. "Like a
mighty army moves the church of God."

The church must constantly be a stream of human
tendency and allow the flow of the Gospel full play, which
will ultimately make for righteousness. Stopped, it becomes a
dead sea of moral and spiritual degeneracy. Our Christianity
is a process not a possession.

Spring is nature's salvation. Spring is the time when
nature's God says, "Behold, I will make all things new."
Religion in general, and theology in particular, need the
spring; this is their only salvation. The God of Abraham also
said to the people, "Go forward." Abraham went as a heretic,
but became the father of all the faithful seed. Judaism, at her
best, was the fruit. Jesus spoke, "Moses says, but I say unto
you as much and more." He is the greatest progressive of
history.

Today we have churches crying for the faith once
delivered unto the saints. One preacher said, "The most that
we can do is to raise Cain." Why fear to go forward? Will
science disprove your narrow concepts? Fear of science
reveals a fatal lack of faith. This, in itself, is a deadly sin. God
and truth are secure. Christ had to confess that there were
many things He had to say, but they could not bear them
then. Let us as children of light welcome every gleam of
intelligence, every fact or suggestion, that may throw added
light upon the multiplying mysteries of life and destiny.

"Behind the dim unknown
Standeth God within the shadow,
Keeping watch above His own."

We have said, "Platitudes will not suffice." We also know that visions are easily painted, utopias are gilded dreams of good men, prophets have built golden eras of rest and plenty, and poets have sung empires into perfect justice and equality. Today we need more, we need united hearts called brotherhood. All the visions, dreams, and utopias are futile without this spirit. This was needed by the children of Israel to go forward; not theories, legislation, not even organization, but rather moral push, with a spiritual fire. They needed to discard the backward look, inertia, divisions, and get into battle array.

Christianity is a going concern if Christians are "going on into perfection," both in the knowledge of truth and in its practices, unto the measure of the stature of the fullness of Christ. I reassert that Christendom needs most of all not a pogrom but a program, not priests but prophets, not pillars but pathfinders, pioneers going over paths never traveled by theologians; not that our theology asks us to believe too much, but rather too little. We say that the better a thing is, the truer it is. Predicate that about God and it is absolutely incontestable.

Truth is worthless in solution or splendid in isolation. It must be brought from the abstract to the concrete, from the supernumerary to the effective relation. I venture to say that if this were done, we would begin now to practice what we preach, to behave as we believe. We would furnish an outstanding sensation for a sensation-sated world. It would be news, headline news. There would be no room for anything else. All forms of evil would be starved off the stage. In the words of Robert Browning:

"Man is not God—but hath God's end to serve,
A Master to obey, a courage to take.
Somewhat to cast off and somewhat to become;
Grant this, then, man must pass from old to new,
From vain to real, from mistake to fact,
From what once seemed good, now proved best;
How could man have progression otherwise?"

WHY HAVE A RELIGION?

Text: "Behold we have forsaken all and followed Thee; what shall we have therefore?"
—Matthew 19:27

This is a practical age when everything is examined and valued. Our pragmatic minds investigate every institution, custom, creed, and form. There are concrete answers when we ask, "Why business?" The answer immediately is, "To make a living." "Why law?" "To keep order and harmony in society." "Why art?" "To make life beautiful." "Why religion? What pressing need does it supply? What does it profit a man today? Life is short and rich with opportunities, then why be concerned if religion is incidental to life?" Impulsive Peter asked, "We have forsaken all, what do we get out of it?"

Religion makes great demands upon its adherents. There is a demand for time and money, and for loyalty and character. Without religion, what would be lost to human welfare, human happiness? It is a difficult question because we have never been without a religion. Religion has endured through time and is universal and instinctive like hunger, thirst, and sex. It is as old as the fetish and ancestral worship. It is embedded in every event and tragedy of life. It is the blending of emotions and aspirations revealing groping hands and broken hearts. When religion is banished in one form, it is recreated in another—transcend it in one age and it is resurrected the next. If it slumbers it never dies; when crushed to earth it rises again. Religion is the supreme passion of the human soul and as changeless as the cradle and the grave. It is as eternal as the heavens that confound us in mystery. It is the whole atmosphere of life; the foundation of character.

58

Our question must be answered in its own sphere. We are not asking what we can expect from the minister or from the church. Religion is not confined to ecclesiasticism. The mechanical aspects of religion fail because of dependence upon management. The ministry demands diplomacy, courage, hard thinking, administrative ability, insight, and foresight; consequently there are great failures in our midst—the ideal exists only in fiction and in utopia. Someone has described the ideal preacher as "never being too long, either in sermons or prayers; he never forgets what he ought to remember nor remembers what he ought to forget; he knows just when to speak and when to be silent; he is educated enough to be a college president and unassuming enough to be a humble beginner; he never has any financial embarrassments as he always manages to live comfortably on the smallest salary; he never quarrels but is always outspoken and courageous; he is at once an ideal visitor and an ideal student; his theology is old fashioned enough to please the most conservative and new-fangled enough to please the most radical; there is never any trouble in placing him as any church would be glad to have his ministry. This ideal minister found a church but could not remain, because of an imperfect congregation. They wanted a man to think as they thought but they did not think alike."

Let us dismiss the organization and the management, and analyze the philosophy of religion. Man is, as Sabatier declared, "incurably religious." Research and meditation may clarify and broaden our idea of God, but the fact is, that man believes in some sort of Higher Power as naturally and inevitably as he accepts the evidence of his sense, and believes in a world outside himself. Seneca said: "Call Him what you please, either nature or fate or fortune, they are all the self-same God who diversely useth His divine providence." When asked, "Why have a religion?" my only answer is that philosophy and science can give only implications; but the uncontroverted and indisputable argument is that man has always believed. God manifests Himself to man, immediately in man's soul and indirectly through nature and history. Of course, the varieties of manifestations are innumerable and different to each individual. A Frenchman wrote, "God made man and since that time man has been making God." Religion is universal and needs no justification. The underlying nature of this universal experience, however, and its manifold expressions or forms, may profitably be studied. The ideas, feelings, and conduct involved in religion may be investigated, and one set of experiences may be compared with another. Then we ask, "Why have a religion?"

I want men and women who have to fight the battles of life, those who suffer and die, to look at religion—not as an antiquarian curiosity but as something at the center of throbbing reality. I want them to know the beauty and worth of religion, to know the theology, passion, and practice of the Christ Who exemplified religion and made it the center of life. To Him, it was not a creed, ecclesiasticism, ordinance or miracle—it was life. John 10:10, "I am come to give you life and give it abundantly."

If religion is life, then what is life? Biologists and psychologists say it is drives, wants, wishes, urges. Let us limit our discourse to the two fundamentals. First, the UNIVERSAL URGE TO KNOW—from youth to age, we want to know. To gain knowledge is to add to life. We begin by asking, "whence, whither, how, when, where, who, why?"We seek light and truth. Over every university we could write in life's blood: "We want a working philosophy of life. Tell us, is this a friendly universe? Am I a creature of blind chance? Am I in the throes of struggle with a heartless machine? Why am I here? Whence my entrance? Whither my exit? What is truth? Why live? Why struggle?"

In our inquiry, we discover that the darkest mystery lies closest to what is best understood. Herbert Spencer wrote: "The religious sense is nothing but the sense of mystery. Religion is only the recognition of the incomprehensibility which is at the heart of all things. It is awe in the presence of this mystery." I know that religious literature throughout the world and in all ages, sooner or later, gives utterance to this thought. This is the cry of Tertullion: 'It is credible because it is foolish. It is certain because it is impossible." The ancients cried that science was born of wonder and the moderns cry that wonder is born of science. They are both right. We live in the midst of impenetrable mystery after we allow for philosophic speculation. The source, meaning, and destiny of life remain a mystery. Cold logic cannot prove anything nor can it disprove. It must start and end with a hypothesis. Logic simply postpones explanation. Mystery has its place in religion. Spencer is absolutely right but religion is not all mystery. Many times I should like to discharge a religious theme by saying that it is a mystery. I am asked: "Why should I have to endure this useless pain? Why should the innocent suffer for the guilty? Why should error cause more suffering than sin? Why should our heaviest suffering come from mistakes not our fault? Why have all these broken careers? Why premature deaths?" We cannot ignore these pertinent questions asked in the white heat of life. We can make answer to others but not to ourselves. We say that life is to be disciplined, to develop spiritual qualities, and to recognize the law of opposites. We say that God's ways are not our ways; God's thoughts are not our thoughts. David reached the height of religious expression when, tired in body and soul, he said, "The Lord is my Shepherd, I shall not want." Job cried with confidence, "I know that my Redeemer liveth." Paul was beaten and imprisoned when doing his duty; his only offense was preaching the Gospel; but he wrote, "I know in Whom I have believed." Augustine, in the midst of speculation, tormented by insoluble riddles, and bewildered in mind and heart, cried out, "Thou art my God—Most High—Most Good—Most Potent—Most Omnipotent—Most Merciful and Most Just." Robert Louis Stevenson, after twenty years of invalidism, said, "I believe in the ultimate decency of things." Victor Hugh, at death, declared, "Death is not a blind alley; it is a thoroughfare." These men felt the presence of that infinite, incomprehensible power which is in all things, through all things, under all things, and over all things.

We have listened to the utterances of religious souls and we realize their sense of mystery, but there has been something more vital than mystery. There can be no mystery without knowledge. Take away all that we know of any subject and there could be no mystery. Mystery is always mystery of something. There must be knowledge and positive faith at the center. Men may pray to a mystery, but cannot praise it; bring an offering, but cannot trust it; seek to gain its favor, but cannot love it. Praise, trust, and love are at the heart of our religious life. Spencer says they are unknowable but so are matter, force, time, space, and motion. In their last analyses they are unknown; it is the unknown that holds our interest—the mystical union that holds the home together; it is the Divine Christ, not the human Jesus, Who has kept Christianity in the world for the last twenty centuries. We can say that there is a power making for righteousness that is not our own; it upholds the right and confers a blessing upon life. Under its guidance all things work together for good. It produces heroism we call character. Without trials and tribulations, we would not know life nor the meaning of character. I have not defined religion because a definition is a limitation and distinguishes it from other things. When the object defined is complex, intricate, vague and vast, points of view will be numerous and definitions will vary. I said it was the Universal Urge to Know that tells why we have a religion. A definition of religion will exclude more than it includes; it shuts out more than it shuts in.

> "Flower in the crannied wall,
> I pluck you out of the crannies—
> Hold you here, root and all, in my hand,
> Little flower—but if I could understand
> What you are, root and all, and all in all
> I should know what God and man is."

If we cannot understand a tiny flower, need one marvel at the diversity of opinions respecting religion?

The Second URGE IS TO BE. Life is more than knowing something; it is also being something. We need direction, but we also need power to travel in that direction. We need something that will keep us from losing our way, but likewise from losing heart. We need to face the facts of life. We need also power to conquer them. When the angel of death stops at our home, or when injustice sweeps down upon us, when misunderstanding and error condemn us, we need more than Henley's humanism: "masters of our fate and captains of our souls." We need moral reserve, soul sufficiency, and spiritual uplift. We need beneath us the everlasting arms. We need the religion of Jesus Christ. After all, the real essence of our Christian religion is not being, but *becoming*. It is not attaining, but pursuing. The spirit striving for the power of becoming, satisfies deeper impulses that are understood only in the soul. It is the experience Wordsworth had as he gazed about Tintern Abbey and felt.

"A presence that disturbed me with a joy
Of elevated thought—a sense sublime
Of something far more deeply interfused."

Proof of this can only be found in experience. It is the experience we have all had standing at the grand canyon, or looking at the Arizona sunset or the night view of Old Faithful geyser in Yellowstone Park, or finding a spiritual vision from a line of poetry or the strain of a Beethoven melody. It is also the love of a soul that is willing to lay down its life for a friend; a mother silently watching and praying by the bedside of a dying child; the saint listening to conscience; the seer catching the vision of a pure desire; the martyr, dying for an ideal.

This is religion, a great supreme emotion, rolling over troubled spirits like the cleansing power of the waves of the sea, that gives rest. It is beyond sight and physical sense. It is embracing the teachings, example, and devotion of Christ. In

Him I am anxious for nothing; in Him I find prayer for everything and through Him I am thankful for anything. We sing:

> "O're moor and fen
> O'er crag and torrent
> Till the night is gone."

MORE THAN LIFE

Text: "Whosoever shall lose his life for My sake shall find
it."
Matthew 16:25

In our Chapel Service we have just sung the words,
"more than life to me," from Fanny Crosby's old hymn,
"Pass Me Not, O Gentle Savior." Is there anything more than
life? Isn't life everything? We are not asking like Rodin's,
"The Thinker," "What is life?" We are not going to
philosophy, psychology, theology, or biology to define it.
Someone has said, "If you think about life, you laugh; if you
feel life intensely, you cry." I know some consider it a
comedy, others a tragedy, and still others—that it is an
emotional spree or a bloodless struggle for survival. When you
ask, "Why do I exist?" the best minds reply, "Because you
exist."

One man says that life is mechanical; it is physical—when
you have health, exuberance, appetite, passion, you have life.
Another says that life is mental—"My mind to me a
kingdom is,"—it is logic, imagination, conversation, creative
thinking. There are as many answers as there are individuals.
Buddha would say, "Be nothing, annihilate self." Nietzsche,
in his "Will to Power" said, "Assert yourself, be a superman."
Ecclesiastes says, "Vanity of vanities, all is vanity,"—that is,
you do not find life in wealth, fame, position or wisdom. The
Master of Life gave the only answer we can accept: "Lose
your life for My sake and the Gospel's and find life." He said
to the rich young ruler, "Go, sell, give and live."

If the only way to find life is to lose it and give it, is
there anything more? A number of years ago, a play made
Broadway and enjoyed a long run there, which is remarkable
in itself—"Death Takes A Holiday." In the play, death takes

65

the form of a man and goes forth to see what men think of him. On this holiday leave, nothing dies. Nature and human nature survive. Death everywhere discovers that men fear him. I have frequently said that men will borrow, bribe, steal, or kill, to keep life. Whether they are old or young, rich or poor, educated or ignorant, sick or well, the first law and the last law of life is self-preservation. When a benefactor wishes to be remembered he gives to benevolences to prolong life. In pain, sorrow, and certain death, a man will fight for his life and die fighting for it. The invalid concludes with everyone else–"Life is too brief, life is sweet." In the light of these unalterable facts, is there something more than life?

The Apostle Paul said, "Life is dear," but it was not dear to him. He was mobbed in Ephesus, and dragged through the streets for dead; taken to the judgment seat of Gallio in Corinth and falsely accused; imprisoned and flogged in Philippi; shipwrecked and stoned and left for dead. Afterward, he wrote to the Corinthians: "In labors more abundant, in stripes above measure, in prisons more frequent, in deaths oft, in journeyings in perilous waters, in subjection to robbers and in the hands of heathens, I was not disobedient unto the heavenly vision–I count not my life dear unto myself."

Duty is more than life. The boys in Viet Nam know it is the greatest word in our language. I have been criticised for emphasizing duty even above love, but we all know there is a great deal of religious sentiment that goes under the name of love. Duty is a robust, august, majestic word, with nobility. "What ought I to do?" has been back of every Christian issue. "What must I do?" is asked by every Christian who declares that faith without works is dead. Our civilization quakes from center to periphery, not because of a cosmic catastrophe; but because we have done what we should not have done, and have left undone the things we should have done. Oliver Wendell Holmes must have spoken to our generation when he said, "Christianity is not the rudder that steers the ship, but simply the flag which the nations fly at the masthead." Because we neglect our duty we lose confidence in our Gospel and in ourselves.

Duty is more than wish, desire, or feeling. It has priority right in our lives. It is the binding force which declares, "Do right at all cost." This implies faith, conscience, and loyalty. Lowell cried:

"Do thy duty; that is best
Leave unto the Lord the rest."

A young man says, "My duty is to make a success of life." To him this means increased production, economic power, material surplus. These factors make for moral progress to be sure, but he often misses the mark by confusing the means of living with the ends of life. Duty also carries with it justice. The Russian youth says: "I, too, live with duty: I have obligations to the proletariat and the class welfare of my state; I have a duty to advance the organic society, security, growth, and glory." Duty also carries with it respect. Anything that suppresses personal freedom, stunts the moral growth, regiments or eradicates religion is categorically wrong.

Followers of the Christ have a duty to keep the church from becoming an asylum for Christian refugees and an army defeated by paganism. We are followers of men who turned the world upside down and from that heritage we will never depart. Nelson, at the battle of Trafalgar, with an empire hanging in the balance and great issues at stake, flung to the breeze his message to the sailors of the British fleet— "England expects this day that every man will do his *duty.*" When Nehemiah was building the wall, the enemies without and within were ridiculing, scorning, and cursing him; he shouted back, "Should such a man as I flee?" There was a call of duty, and Nehemiah made his answer. Frequently we hear, too often to tell, of the captain who would not leave his ship but go down with her.

"So nigh is grandeur to our dust
So near is God to man
When duty whispers low, 'Thou must,'
Then youth replies, 'I can'."

Another word more than life is *Others.* The Master of
life said, "I am come not to be ministered unto but to
minister and give my life a ransom for many." Saving life, we
lose it; losing life, we save it. Over and above the elements of
money, power, honor, luxury, is unselfish devotion. Service
above self is the sacrificial use of life. It is commonplace to
tell of mothers who gave themselves unhesitatingly for their
children. The blood of the martyrs has always been the seed
of the church. Life must be magnetized, and the whole of life
must be drawn to a cause greater than self. Where there is
reservation, there is remorse. We see this in the labor
movement today; everything is secondary to the cause. The
scientist has always demonstrated it, by going to the bowels
of the earth, the stratosphere, the mountain top, the ocean
depth, for discovery and truth. Life is secondary. The goal
must intrigue and must be reached. A man arrives only when
he finds something bigger and better to do. This is the
paradox: the greater his search, the greater the search
becomes. To direct attention and interest inwardly is to
exhaust one's best self. The self-absorbed person is not only
enervating himself; he is on the way to neurosis.

What better example can we have than the Cross? The
Master did not pray for Himself. He prayed for others,
"Father, forgive them!" He began His ministry by ministering; He ended by giving; and when men realize this, they
can understand the centurion who passed by the Cross and
said, "Truly this Man was the Son of God." The follower of
Christ switches self-pity to compassion for others, he turns
concern from self to society, he makes self-importance less
than the dignity of mankind.

One of the most renowned characters of service was
General "Chinese" Gordon. His life is the personification of

unselfishness. There are three monuments to him. One is in Trafalgar Square with the worn sad face turned toward the help which never came. The story of "too little and too late" is not new in our missionary endeavors. Then there is the magnificent inscription in St. Paul's, London:

> Major General Charles George Gordon, C. B.
> who at all times
> and everywhere gave his strength
> to the weak
> his substance to the poor
> his sympathy to the suffering
> his heart to God.

The third monument is the life-sized figure of him seated on a dromedary in the garden in Khartoum, where, sorely pressed by an overwhelming, superior force, he was faithful unto death. The face of Gordon is not turned toward the Nile by which he could have escaped; it is turned toward the great desert whose cry for help he heard, and to which he attempted to respond. "Greater love hath no man than this."

Finally, more than life, is *Jesus Christ.* "For me to live is Christ, to die is gain." The idea of finding life by cross-bearing, by self-denial, is far removed from our thinking and practice. Rather do we boast of abundant living with ease and comfort. Any antidote, religious or otherwise, finds a tremendous following. We seek short hours of labor and the de luxe in everything. We want less demanding of effort, with fewer restrictions on desires and impulses. We want the Cross of Christ for decoration, symbols, and in a figurative sense. We enjoy the Christianity of the priest rather than that of the prophet. The priest brings the sacraments, worship, and personal ministry; the prophet rebukes the sin and the sinner; he condemns the nation and indicts civilization. We enjoy Chrisitanity when it makes us feel self-satisfied, complacent, and good. We reject it when it convicts us of sin, shows us our evil ways, and calls us to repentance. When religion demands the Cross, we walk with Him no more.

Christianity alone preaches the Cross. Buddha shunned death until he was eighty; Confucius and Zoroaster did not conceive of the idea of sacrificing themselves for the good of others. Mohammed established his religion by killing rather than by being killed. Only One gave Himself to redeem men from sin; he laid down His life that others might have abundant life, eternal life.

Before He died, He lived. I remember our philosophy professor shouting: "Nietzsche says, 'Live dangerously.' This brutal philosopher had something. Christians must do it." As I have tried to interpret Christianity, I cannot think of anything more dangerous to attempt. It is not easy to love one's enemies in a world in which your enemies scheme to take advantage of you; it is difficult to forgive seventy times seven, when people are indifferent to your forgiveness of them; it is almost impossible to refrain from being anxious for tomorrow, when organized forces are working for their interest, not yours; yet, in these things Christ calls us to duty, service, and sacrifice.

Tradition tells us that Leban was to marry the daughter of Joseph, Jesus' brother. Leban asked Mary, the mother of Jesus, what He had taught. Mary answered: "He taught men to forgive one another; to make life easy for others rather than self; to formulate a principle for life and never sacrifice it regardless of the cost; to be willing to die for the faith that is in you; not to be afraid of those who kill the body, but rather, the soul. When you degrade or dishonor human life, you degrade and dishonor God." Leban asked Mary, "Has anyone· ever really tried to live as He taught?" Mary answered, "I do not think so." Then Leban replied, "It would be interesting to see what would happen if they did."

"Who answers Christ's insistent call
Must give himself, his life, his all;
Christ claims him wholly for His own.
He must be Christ's, and Christ's alone."

MYSTERY IN RELIGION

Texts: "Verily, Thou art a God that hidest Thyself."
—Isaiah 45:15
"Canst thou by searching find out God?"
—Job 11:7

The oldest book in the Bible asks the question, "Canst thou by searching find out God?" Who can presume to understand God or know Him? The essence of His being is an impenetrable mystery, yet belief in God is the foundation of religion. The question of God's existence cannot be faced without atheism. It is the hiding God that makes atheism possible. If the astronomer with his telescope or the physicist with his microscope could reveal the habitation of God there would be no atheism. Paul declared, "We see through the glass darkly."

The first mystery that confronts man is man. He thinks of the physical evil in the world, the ravages of disease and the blind destructive forces; he considers the moral evil in the world, the violence and cruelty of man. The inevitable question arises, "How can there be moral evil in a world ruled by a good God?" The thinking man asks why a world ruled by a good God should not have been made perfect—if this omnipotent goodness reigned, religion would not be necessary. Man has sought the good life, and the world has mocked at his dream. He has always had to fight his way up through adversity, disease, tragedy, and daily encounter with pain, fear, sorrow, defeat, and death. In ancient Babylon the people decided that gods kept life for themselves and to man gave death.

The monotheist, believing in one God, has a problem: to be God, God has to be almighty, all-wise and all-good. In Isaiah 45:6 and 7, we read; "I am the Lord and there is none

71

else. I form the light and create darkness. I make peace and create evil. I, the Lord, do all these things." The traveling evangelists endeavor to answer. They tell us that evil is of the devil and the good is from God. If God cannot control the devil, then the devil is God's equal. If God can control the devil and does not, then God is not good. We may enlarge upon the facts of injustice and suffering of the innocent. We see the frequent prosperity of the unscrupulous and the poverty of the moralist.

Our first question arises: not, "How can we believe in God?" but, "How can we believe in man?" Think of the physical evil man could prevent, if he would. Think of the poverty, the war, the man-made misery; think of the moral evil that man could help to destroy and the social injustice he could end, if he would. We believe in man in spite of these dreadful evils. Man is struggling against them and fighting to refrain from them. History is written by man fighting for the good against the evil in himself and in the world. The essence of theology is the endless combat of the GOOD in the universe against the EVIL in the universe. The battle is far from being won.

In view of all this evil, will we say that God is not real? Is it not more sensible to say that it is our definition of God that is not real? The supreme mystery of the universe and of faith is not how we can reconcile belief in God with a world full of cruelty and wrong. This is how we *can* believe in God in such a world. He is a struggling God, as H. G. Wells says in "Mr. Britling Sees It Through." We are to fight on His side, on the side of the good. This is practical religion: to fight with God against the evil in the world, against disease, against cruelty, against ignorance, and against barbarism and injustice. This is the mystery, a good God in an evil world. I am not evading the issue. I confess I know no answer nor anyone who has complete knowledge. It remains a paradox. Paradox is written into every phase of life. The hindrance to all motion is friction and without friction there could be no motion. The only way to get power is through repose and repose is contrary to power. We get knowledge by giving attention and concurrently by ignoring. In psychology we call it assimilation, while simultaneously using discrimination; adding to and subtracting from; ascertaining likenesses and at the same time differences. There once was a song called, "I Am Remembering To Forget." In a more philosophic trend, William James speaks of "the everlasting struggle to keep unchanged the tendency to renovate." This is the mystery of life, its final analysis is in the paradox. It is God's sovereignty and man's free will—a good God in an evil world.

The second great mystery is the existence of God. Who has seen Him, or heard Him, or knows Him? We are asked to believe in a Being of Whom we know nothing. The Scripture confirms this, "Canst thou by searching find out God?" We see what we think are His traces, the effect of His power in nature and in man. What do we really know of God? What is He? We do not comprehend the mystery of His existence. Why then, should man believe in His being? We may ask, "Why believe in man?"

Man knows no more about himself than he knows of God. Man is not body that obeys his will. He has senses to see, a voice to speak; he commands them but they are not man. Man is a mystery! He sends a message along a telegraph wire called a nerve; the central station is called brain, and one hundred and fifty pounds move and obey. How? Nobody knows. Man's voice agitates the air waves and the brain translates them into thoughts. How? Nobody knows.

Man is also a chemical factory. He takes in fuel and it is separated mysteriously into gastric juices, into bile, into pancreatic fluid, into thyroid extract, into blood, into lymph, into nerve energy, into vital energy, into the dynamic power of speech, of thought, of will, of action. Modern laboratories cannot begin to equal men as chemical factories. Think of changing fuel into force; force into moral fire and the light of

the mind, and the tremendous urge of action. The prime
mover of all of this—*man*—what is man? We do not know. I
know that man is a living, breathing, rational being, filling
space. I also know he is an unsolvable mystery. I cannot
understand man; why should I expect to understand God? I
have never seen God. We are told that God is Spirit. I have
never seen man—man is spirit. You say, "But here is man's
body and we know something of its function in the
circulation of blood, digestion and development." I see this
infinite universe with its planets, the ebb and flow of the sea,
the change of seasons, balanced cosmic forces, the law of
gravitation and the daily cycles of darkness and light. "Some
call it evolution, others call it God." Man is a mystery with
self-expression; God is a cosmic expression, a mystery.

> "It is not wisdom to be only wise
> And on the inward vision close the eyes
> But it is wisdom to believe the heart."
> —George Santayana

The third mystery I will mention is the use of power which
we do not understand. I push a switch, there is light where
there was darkness. The switch allowed the electric current to
operate. It passed through the carbon filament. Resistance to
the current heated it into incandescence. What is the current?
No one knows. Some say it is the escape of negative
electrons. What are negative electrons? No one knows. Here is
an electric motor. I pull a switch—it begins operation equal to
thousands of man power. It is titanic power, but what?

Whether there be astronomical wonder or terrestrial
marvel, the telescope or the microscope only add to the
mystery. All matter has been revolutionized into tremendous
activity. To add to the mystery, try to read Millikan, Pupin,
Compton, Jeans and the others. Atoms are small solar
systems, with central nuclear electrons running about in an
orbit going faster than a bullet. We have the X-ray. It is X
because it is an unknown quantity, yet the X-ray is helping to

cure disease, particularly fighting cancer. It is also used in horticulture. It is a mystery. A grain of sand has molecular arrangement that calls for mathematics very few, if any, can decipher. A speck of dust cannot be given full chemical or algebraic formula. It is a mystery. If we cannot understand the finite why should we expect to understand the infinite?

We are in a pragmatic age where science contends nothing is true unless proven; nothing happens to a person unless it has been experienced. In this case, Shakespeare is meaningless, "There are more things in heaven and earth, Horatio, than are dreamed of in your philosophy." The more man learned as he looked up, looked out, and looked in and around, the greater the knowledge, but the greater the mystery. Science reveals only further to conceal. First, man had wonder, then inquiry, then knowledge, then greater wonder.

To know a father the child must grow. To know God we would have to be God. The limited cannot understand the illimitable, the human the divine, the temporal the eternal, or the fallible the infallible. To know art, we must be artists; or to know music, we must be musicians. The more perfect we become, greater are the flaws we can detect. The perfect is impossible to man. He is limited to time and space. It is these mysteries that stimulate the imagination and give mystery to our quest for God, omnipotent, omniscient and omnipresent. This is the Infinite Power we call "Father."

Let not the mystery of God repel us from religion. On the contrary, there is challenge and an inspiration in mystery. It questions our intelligence; it awakens the poetic instinct; it stimulates the imagination. Man is forever fascinated by the mysteries of life that have developed the spirit of mysticism in religion.

We want more than abstract concepts of God, man, atomic energy; we want more than a symbol we find in

Moses, Isaiah, and Jeremiah; we want a revelation like Him Who said, "He that hath seen Me, hath seen the Father." When we want the most of the mystery we turn to the incarnation. The Christ did not rebel against the universe and its laws. He called the Absolute, "Father," and we know a father does not nurse weaklings. God is producing great souls. A dangerous life is the only one worth having. Man wants to encounter danger but he wants to believe there is power that is backing him up. If he meets with defeat he does not want abandonment.

Let us keep our profound regard for science, and keep our mystical nature stimulated with belief in, and aspirations to, the world's growing knowledge. This does not mean superstition, but rather faith in the unseen. The soul is lifted in conceptions of something higher than the world can give. It will give life transfiguration into the higher elements that are eternal in the heavens.

George W. Briggs has written:

"Lord of all majesty and might,
Whose presence fills the unfathomed deep;
Wherein uncounted worlds of light,
Through countless vigils keep;
Eternal God, can such as we,
Frail mortal men, know ought of Thee?

Beyond all knowledge Thou art wise,
With wisdom that transcends all thought;
Yet still we seek with straining eyes,
Yea, seek Thee as our fathers sought;
Nor will we from the quest depart,
Till we shall know Thee as Thou art."

THE KING OF KINGS

Text: "The King of Kings and Lord of Lords."
—I Timothy 6:15

In a church with democratic policy, can we proclaim a spiritual leader as a King? In a government with only a collection of doctrines, ceremonies, and rituals, can we have a Lord of Lords? We know man is so constituted that he must have a master. It is natural to seek guidance and authority; every tribe has a chieftain. The church naturally turned to Rome, because of its central power, both political and ecclesiastical. Man has always sought an absolute, an infallibility. The eminent scientist, Thomas Huxley, said he would gladly be wound up as a clock, if, in doing so, he could operate without flaw or weakness. Man calls for a master, be that master a person, a principle, or a passion. We say, "Better a bad ruler than no ruler at all." The Old Testament tells us that there was a time when "Every man did that which was right in his own eyes." This is the danger of liberty; it becomes license, and ends in a collapsed character. Henry Churchill King says, "The first duty of every soul is to find, not its freedom, but its master."

We do not want a master unless he incarnates the power of truth, conveying healing and health to human souls, and not by mental abstractions. We have had many religious leaders but only one Christ. His message is our chief spiritual treasure, and that message is inseparable from His personality. To us, in a real and not a dogmatic sense, "The truth is in Jesus." This is the Word becoming flesh and the truth revealed through character.

Why follow a peasant who lived twenty centuries ago? We preach first hand contact with God. Why have a king in a democracy? The answers are evident. Truly understood, we do not have perfect freedom, but only within the law. The difference between democracy and autocracy, or between a fraternal and an ecclesiastical church, is that in the former the leader is a servant, while in the latter the leader is a tyrant. Democracy believes in the contagion of character and the leaven of beneficial leadership. The greater and truer the leader, the fuller the life of the society he serves. In these terms, Christ is the world's first and finest democrat. He came, "not to be ministered unto, but to give His life as a ransom." We follow the "King of Hearts," to use Bishop Fulton Sheen's title for Christ, not as slaves driven to obedience by the lash of authority, not as believers in an infallible pope, but as His free disciples, who learn from Him the secret of disinterested service and unselfish love. Congregations say to pastors when they are installed in a church, "We will follow you as long as you follow the Master." This matter of discipleship transcends all theories; the lesser is bound to the greater; the smaller souls gravitate to the larger. Emerson reminds us that he who has more soul conquers. Those who refuse the leadership of the King of Kings follow some ruling power somewhere. We have seen men turn from Christ but they have turned to Lenin, Hitler, or Castro, led by souls mightier than they. The New Testament Christ is not a mass of superstitions, ecclesiastical creeds, or traditional dogma; but the exalted Spirit leading in divine love, which is never too high for the lowly, and never too low for the wise and learned. This King is that progressive, continuous revelation, which is limited to the mentality of no one age and is the exclusive keeping of no one sect or creed.

What qualities characterize a real constitutional king? First, he must be born, not made; he must be conscious of his authority and prerogative; he must be dedicated to the highest good for the greatest number. Examining the King of character, we find He is Master in the realms of INTELLECT, MORALS, AND RELIGION. Christ had no money, He was King but used no legislative program, He had no influential friends, He had practically no organization. He created no corporate mass movement; yet in three short years He launched the most revolutionary, deep-spread, forward movement the world has ever seen or known. "Never man spake like this man." After centuries of mental research and development, the intellectual genius of Christ remains a mystery. Its vitality, its sanity, its lucid purity, its grandeur, and the capacity to think universally and concretely, continue to dazzle us. Today His intellectual power surpasses the practical reason of the father of modern philosophy, Immanuel Kant, the intuitive mind of Bergson, and the pragmatic utilitarianism of William James. The mind of Christ means to the student: His insight and foresight, His outlook, His motive, His thought, His knowledge and the revelation He made of character values. It was God-centered. Everything far and near, great and small, the crash of empires, or the fall of a sparrow, was a revelation of God. Nothing in His thought was separate from God.

Yet, with all of this, He was without formal education. Without scientific dictum which was a limitation of that age, and without the distinction of a discoverer or an inventor, He spoke as one having authority. He died at an early age, and on a Roman cross, despised, rejected, scorned, and spat upon—the Teacher of Teachers, standing solitary and unapproachable, not only in mind, but in heart. Christians cannot understand His intellectual genius until, and unless, they live with Him, love Him, obey Him, study His words, brood over His life—that they may come to think of God, of man, of life, as He did. It is thus we pray, "In the Name of Christ, our Lord." We ask for the things He would ask. Speaking as a minister preaching to the intellect, there must be the ability to meet the shifting ideas, to meet the conditions and demands of life. If the message is Christ-centered, the minister will ward off incredulity, sluggishness, prepossession, misguided piety, and apply himself to the task of resolute thinking. It is heresy to fear the truth. The Christian intellect maintains the purification of scholarly wisdom. It does not despise culture for the sake of religion, neither does it set aside religion for the sake of culture. It is mandatory for us to remember that true culture is not conceived in the wits but in the souls of men (Colossians 2:3–"in Whom are hid all the treasures of wisdom and knowledge"), for all generations. Carlyle avowed that he who mastered the first forty-seven propositions of Euclid stood nearer to God than he did before that achievement. The most accomplished scholar is the one educated at the feet of Jesus in the college of fishermen.

More than intellect, Christ is unexcelled in the elements of morals and in ethical culture. In the popular mind there is much confusion respecting the relation between religion and morals. Christ was a moral philosopher and distinguished between right and good. Right conduct is conformity to rules. The Pharisees had six hundred and thirteen Levitical laws, but He asked if they were directed to a useful purpose. Conduct directed toward the supreme good is good conduct. Christ instructed men that motives are as consequential as conduct. Righteousness is doing one's duty from right motives, and fidelity to obligations is adorned by the attractive graces of unselfishness, sociability, and kindness. In our modern world we would say that if the moral man gave to the poor to get votes, if he were chaste only because he feared indulgence of passion might injure his business by ruining his reputation, if his motive was bad, we could not call him a good man. We all know men are often outwardly good for selfish ends. They are trusted only when they are believed to be good at heart, as well as good in deed. "Out of the heart flow the issues of life."

In the moral realm, Christ alone is sinless. He is pre-eminent, supreme, flawless, and fleckless, pure as the white light of heaven. This is the only biography where we do not have a cry for forgiveness, yet we read, "He was tempted, like all men." He stands a towering mountain peak, with its perennial crown of snow, standing in majesty and glory against the azure sky.

In one lecture, Dr. Fosdick began, "Lecky, in his 'History of European Morals' says: 'The simple record of Christ's three short years of active life has done more to regenerate and soften mankind than all the disquisitions of philosophers and the exhortations of moralists'." The Unitarian theologians call this the Divinity of Christ. It is the moral concept raised to a divine standard. In our Christian study, we believe it is the God-consciousness in His soul. It is the recognition of God as the Divine Father, as the source of all goodness. "Why call Me good? There is none good but the Father." Nature and man find their unity and only explanation in the eternal God.

Christ is the King of Kings in the realm of Religion. He is a fact apart, a phenomenon unequalled, a manifestation without a second. Let me say cautiously, He is Man and superman. He touches all, yet He is above all. Religion, at its best, refuses to be satisfied with exclusively human categories relative to Him. His character, His claims, and His effects are unique. Literature, art, civilization, and centuries rise up to do Him reverence, a King in intellect, in morals, but the King of Kings in religion. Through Him, God speaks, in Him, man hopes. We have religious leaders by the score; but whether it is the world leaders in religions, such as Moses, Buddha, Confucius, Mohammed, or the others, none of them has presented the world such claims either God-ward or man-ward as those of Christ. He makes the vital kinship with God the medium of His full and final revelation of God. It was a new day in the history of religion when Jesus made this revelation the fundamental and constructive concept in religion. He taught the disciples the meaning of being a King; it was the Father's Kingdom, and not that of a monarch. He taught them to live as children, not as subjects, and as brothers, not as patricians or plebeians. Whe He spoke, it was as representing the Father; when He wrought, He did the Father's works; when He suffered, it was the Father's glory; and when He died, it was to the Father He prayed. In all of His teachings there is not a hint of monarchical monotheism:

"I am a King." Instead, He said, "My Kingdom is not of this world." Christ refused the King's sword and accepted the godly crown.

This is our Christianity: it is inspiration, not legislation; it is the educator's method, not the executive's—not law, but love. This is what our Christian faith declares: The Kingdom Christ is to rule must do, and be; trust God with complete reliance; obey His laws and face life's dangers with courage; believe that the King of Kings is Lord of death as He is the Savior of mankind.

"Were the whole realm of nature mine,
That were a present far too small;
Love so amazing, so divine
Demands my soul, my life, my all."

WORSHIP IS A SPIRITUAL EXPERIENCE

Text: "The true worshiper shall worship the Father in spirit and in truth."

—John 4:23

No passage within the compass of the Bible opens our subject with words of such liberality and power as the words of our text. They were spoken to the woman of Samaria near Jacob's well. The purpose of the church is to train and feed the spirit of worship, not only with hymns and prayers and instruction, but to stimulate and refresh the feelings of wonder and awe. There must be a feeling of gratitude, trust, and obligation to the Father in heaven. Worship must appeal to the aesthetic; it must be moral as well as beautiful.

The spirit of adoration is as old as the record of history. Men and women have always worshipped from the dawn of time to the present hour. They have worshiped in fear and in exultation of spirit; they have worshiped by means of the frailest formulations of breath—words—and in deep silence. They have worshiped in their strength and in their weakness, in their sorrow, and in their joy. The Scriptures open with the dramatic quest. Adam heard the voice of God in the garden. Abel offered sacrifice to an unseen power; and the guilty Cain bowed with his gift, though it was not accepted. Before recorded history, we have implications of pagan worship and we have the authentic history of ruined temples and their solemn traditions.

Across the years, we have had an endless procession of warriors, statesmen, scholars, laborers, poets, and artists, all moving in worship forms before their gods. Plutarch observed: "If we traverse the world, it is possible to find cities without walls, without letters, without wealth, without schools; but never a city without a temple or altar for worship." Men have worshiped under the open sky, in groves or forests, in mosques and pagodas, in temples and cathedrals, and in meeting houses. They have engaged the smoke of sacrifice or the silence of the Quaker group. They have worshiped the sun, the moon, the stars. They have bowed before sticks and stones, cows, and monkeys, even rats. The quest has been universal. They have been seeking light, guidance, protection, production, reproduction, inspiration, from forces greater than their own. It is the human desire to transform, dignify, and lift life out of futility and fear, into health, wealth, and happiness. We may be far removed from the dawn-man, living as we do in cities of steel and cement, with automation, technology, jet propulsion, medical science, computers, and push button gadgets—nevertheless, we, too, worship and still seek. At every cross-road we have our shrine for worship—the name we give it is immaterial.

The disposition to worship belongs to the structure of the human soul. Religious ideas, like those of science and sociology, are changed by progress and diffusion of knowledge. We are creatures of evolution, rising from our dead selves up to higher things. Forms and theories of worship are shattered and left behind by the enlargement and the march of intellect. In spite of rational powers, no definition has been able to give full meaning to the experience of worship. One which is frequently used is, "Worship is the deepest in man yearning for the loftiest in the universe." With the gain of knowledge we instinctively associate the advance of the race. Frequently, men ask, "Will worship be outgrown?" The rationalists often contend that the advance of science will yet eradicate the tendency to prayer and homage. We read of their picture of the globe: "a crust of fossils and a core of fire," spinning in the bleak immensity, and bearing myriads on myriads of intelligent creatures yearly around the sun. This is without wonder, without awe, without a cry from brain or heart into the surrounding mystery!

All religion begins in cosmic emotion. It is the recognition of an essential relationship between the human soul and the great whole of things of which it is the outcome and expression. This we call the cosmic consience. The mysterious universe is always calling and, in some form or other, we are always answering. The artist answers by trying to express his feeling of its beauty; the scientist answers by recognizing its laws and unfolding its wonders; the social reformer answers by his self-denying labor for the common good. In each and every case, there is in the background of experience, a conviction that the unit is the instrument of the ALL. Religion is implied in these and all other activities in which man aims at a Higher-Than-Self. Religion, properly understood, begins when the soul consciously enters upon communion with this Higher-Than-Self as with an all-comprehending intelligence. It is the soul instinctively turning toward that from whence it came. Religion may assume a great many different and even repellent forms but, at bottom, this is what it always is—it is the soul reaching forth to the great mysterious whole of things, the Higher-Than-Self, and seeking for closer communion. We may say the savage with his totem and the Christian at the altar have this in common—they are reaching through the seen to the unseen and the reality beyond. Some contend this is anemic and only a pallid prop upon which to lean—blood, iron, and ruthless might are in the saddle and the four horsemen ride again across the world. It is difficult to read the metropolitan press and not succumb to the lies, hatred, and propaganda of violence which literally fill the air.

In this kind of a world we need some place, somewhere, under the influence of sincere worship, where we may be reassured, not once, but time and time again, that God is not a mirage upon the desert of hate; that this is a moral order; that good will, honor, truth, and righteousness are literally the mightiest forces in the world. The agnostic, H. G. Wells, is on this side; he speaks of "a power that fights with us against the confusion and evil of the world." We need frequently to recall: "Be still and know that I am God." We want an occasional escape into another stratum of reality—something as real as the black panthers and the Viet Nam war. This is standing with the prophets and the philosophers to declare that Jesus is greater than Pilate, Socrates greater than his judges, Schweitzer greater than Hitler, and the peace-makers greater than the war lords. Worship at the Christian altar makes valid for us the eternal power of righteousness, good will and brotherhood.

There are three purposes for which we may study truth—to attain power over nature; to cultivate and enlarge our minds; and to discern and acknowledge a revelation from the boundless and invisible thought. We may study the law of gravitation in all its proofs and applications in order to widen our control over matter. We may study it with equal ardor, without any reference to practical uses, but for the sake of enlarging the domain of truth over which our intellect can sweep. We may study it in relation to this globe and the cosmos—all of this as a disclosure of the thought of an unfathomable Intellect that unfolds itself in the order of the universe. In which of these three ways is the glory of knowledge attained? I say nothing of disparagement of the first two. They are essential to civilization. The last is not inconsistent with devotion. If we stop with the first and second, we miss the highest revelations of truth. We live then in a world of cold effects that never hint at the majesty of their *cause.* It is to refresh men with this noble relationship to truth and knowledge that churches are built. Worship is the exercise which the church is to sustain. All the aspects of truth which will bend the mind of man in humility and exalt it in adoration are legitimately within the range of the pulpit, and are indeed, a portion of its trust. Without the altar for worship the sanctuary is a lecture hall.

One phase of life we cannot overlook, and it is pertinent in Christian worship—we celebrate life together. We cannot survive without society. We are gregarious and only a man in an insane asylum can find satisfaction in solitary confinement. Worship, in a large sense, is corporate. It is mind with mind and spirit with spirit. Man needs companionship to develop his spirituality. In church, which is a fellowship, he shuts himself in so he can shut the world out. When the minister is dull, the music unbearable, and the interior unkempt, even then, in the sanctuary we are compelled to think about loftier ideals than we find in our daily routine. Psalm 122:1, "I was glad when they said unto me, 'Let us go into the house of the Lord'." Habakkuk 2:20, "The Lord is in His holy temple; let all the earth keep silence before Him." Christ went to the temple as His custom was; can we do anything less? Dr. Hocking, head of the department of philosophy in Harvard wrote: "Man needs love, friendship, recreation. Worship is the whole which includes them all." I have worshiped in many synagogues and churches. I endeavor to find expression in the rationalism of Unitarians, the reverence of Episcopalians, the independence of Congregationalists, the enthusiasm of Methodists, the Sunday School training of the Lutherans, the tranquility of the Quakers, the democracy of Baptists, the constitutionalism and discipline of Presbyterians. I confess, at times, I am a spectator rather than a participant. When I go, I have learned to put essentials first—not primarily to hear the preacher or the choir, but to find God in different emphasis. The Roman Catholics can teach us reverence in the sanctuary; they do not go to church, they go to mass, in the celebration or service of the Eucharist. This Church brings them to their knees; we bring the congregation to their feet. I want all the art and artistry, craftsmanship, beauty, culture, and taste we can exercise. To the preacher belongs the responsibility of turning an audience into a congregation.

At the altar, we wait before the beauty, mystery, and tragedy of life. There are so many maladjustments, discords, fears, and worries in the lives of men and women. I do not say that worship alone can smooth out all these things, but it can help to unify our scattered forces. It can bring a certain peace and stability to troubled minds. Here, we bring our hopes and ambitions and hold them up to the light of the ideal. The altar brings us face to face with the great overshadowing mystery and wonder of life. We again express it: "The deepest in man yearning for the loftiest in the universe." All the past is with us. Our mistakes and failures rise before us, our pitiful performances and puny endeavors for the good life haunt us. If it be a sincere worship, out of this celebration of life shall come peace, courage and understanding. It should not be mechanical nor routine, if so, it is not an asset but a liability. Worship is born at times, out of the exalted experiences of life, in the purifying fires of sorrow, in the wonder dawning in the face of a child, in the awe growing out of some magnificent heroic achievement of others–the sheer courage, patience, and faith of men conquering fear, disease, and the shadowy hinterland of the mind. All of these produce moods of worship.

I cannot conclude without including the other half of the miracle wrought at the altar. Worship should give not only peace but also unrest–not only contemplation and a unified individual life, but it should also nourish a hatred against those things which enslave and exploit the bodies and the minds of men. It is easy to withdraw and say that the task of reforming the world is impossible. We are tempted to enter the ivory tower, meditate, and let the world go its wicked way. "What can we do, we are only a few individuals?" Think what a united church front could do! Worship must nerve men's hearts to bring in the Kingdom of Righteousness. This is the most difficult thing in this period of human history. "If thou bring thy gift to the altar and there remember that thy brother hath ought against thee, leave there thy gift before the altar, and go thy way; first be reconciled to thy brother, and then come and offer thy gift." In other words, worship is never an isolated, lone act of ritual or prayer. It is linked with the whole of our activities. It should be a great spring constantly refreshing the drooping faith and flagging spirits in our struggle with the evil of the world. Worship means these specific things to me: a continual assurance of the validity and power of righteousness and good will; it means a healing and strengthening power in the individual; and a dynamic faith by which we face the darkness and evil in the world, unafraid.

THE EMOTIONAL LIFE

Text: "A Man Who told me all things that ever I did."
—John 4:29

I began this topic with an outline on my desk, and over the television came the announcement of two university students, one nineteen years of age, and the other twenty-three years of age, committing suicide in one day. Frankly, I am forced to attempt an analysis of this problem before analyzing the theme that is outlined. Thousands commit suicide annually; it is a national and international problem.

In Isaiah 40:30, 31, we read: "Even the youths shall faint and grow weary, and the young men shall utterly fail; but they that wait upon the Lord shall renew their strength." Isaiah knew that youth could grow weary, and young men could utterly fail. His somber words are realized today. There is hardly a morning when the press does not record another appalling self-slaughter among college students. There are always some unhappy creatures who tire of life. Think of finding them among the strong, with life before them, and with everything to live with and everything to live for—this among the educated class who have learned to reason, to look at life intelligently and logically! These are the ones deserting their flag under the first fire.

The first reaction I have is to ask if education will suffice in meeting life's problems. Apparently it has failed to give moral backbone. Education enlightens, but it does not inspire. Our youth gain in knowledge, but do not gain in strength of character and steadfastness of soul. Education, alone, in this boasted age of progress, is insufficient, and I speak after many years of service with college students. Much more is needed; we plainly see that more discipline than the giving of information is mandatory to meet life as it is and ought to be.

How can education be a panacea for all human ills? How can it be expected to turn weakness into strength, to take the place of moral and religious training, of fine, inspiring traditions, and of a salutary home influence? It is no reflection on education, on its indispensability and its service as the nurse and depository of civilization, to say that it cannot do everything. Instruction alone cannot be omnipotent in its influence.

Something is evidently missing in any system of purely secular education, something, the absence of which, weakens one's power of resistance to morbid and evil influences. What dangerous influences were these two unfortunate weaklings unable to resist? One was the effect of simple suggestion. They read of one suicide, of some student whose will power collapsed; and that suggested another self-slaughter–their own. The power of impluse to blind imitation is not a powerful influence to combat, save when the limited power needed to resist evil suggestions has broken down.

What is it that darkened these young lives, destroyed their desire to live on, and made even the beautiful years of youth seem to them only a dreary ordeal? It has been suggested that the material view of life that considers the universe a soulless machine, depressed and dismayed them– the theory that blind pitiless forces crush the weak and preserve only the strong; and that these forces are careless and indifferent of our merit and demerit. This belief paralyzes the initiative and energy, especially of those who drag behind, who cannot stand the pace, who do not feel equal to the struggle.

There are young men with deadly inferiority complexes, who are full of fears, the nightmare fears of the weak; who think the race is to the swift ·and the battle to the strong. They realize they are neither swift nor strong. What prizes can they win–what material prizes? Can they secure wealth, in a society of mammon-worshipers? Can they achieve power, the only thing in the world that is respected by those who ride roughshod over the weak? If they cannot attain, then why fight on? Why continue being a failure to be pitied?

These are the comments we read in the paper and the remarks made by the commentators. I think more powerful than these positive causes, is the negative reason. What do they lack? Intellectual culture has done its utmost; but how about spiritual culture? Knowledge alone did not stiffen their spines. Their knowledge of natural laws seems to have terrified them. The material theory of the universe has made their little lives appear very poor and worthless. What are they, then, but helpless playthings of the blind, irresistible forces of nature.

Back of reason and reflection are unconscious activities called willing, desiring, striving. The will is often irrational. We do not desire something because we have reflected upon it; we can only find reason after we have desired it; we are not moved by reason, but by desires. Logic never wins a battle.

How about the laws of God, the influence of the Christ Spirit over their spirits, and the infinite over the finite soul? How about faith in an Almighty Power that is not our own, but makes for righteousness? I am not simply speaking of a rival theory of the universe, called humanism, but of something for which the soul of man hungers,—something which it needs and must have, to give value and significance to life, something to furnish an inspiration to us in the common round of daily tasks, as the source and sanction of the best within us.

Without this conviction that the struggle is worth while, that *it is not in vain,* that these divinely appointed duties mean self-fulfillment, self-completion—without this deep divine faith, there is always the danger of despair, even in the heart of the young. They ask, "Is life worth living?" Years ago, the Christian Century magazine carried reviews from philosophers, theologians and men of letters on the same theme, "Is Life Worth Living?" The reaction of atheists led them to a materialistic conclusion that the end is fatalistic, with a mechanistic concept of a soulless determinism. Fatalism, when accepted, is pessimism. The theists expressed an optimism that the end is a beginning. The present discipline is character making, and the ultimate is, to "Be perfect as your Father in Heaven is perfect." Life is divinely controlled and the path leads ultimately onward and upward forever. If one is weak, to be crushed and scrapped, then any prize will not satisfy. The suicides take thought of tomorrow and the next step is too much.

Where are the young to get a spiritual view of life?—(This is our religious ideal.)—from organized religion in a church that is never attended? Absent treatment is meaningless. Medicine can't cure if it remains on the shelf. God speaks to us when we speak to Him. The college, the church, and now the home, have apparently failed. Youth has exhausted the thrills of society and has turned to drugs. In this category we go as low as the 'teen agers. What are we giving to restrain them? What fine, spiritual sense have we awakened in them? What lofty and overmastering ideals have penetrated and gripped them? What has lifted them out of themselves into some great current of unselfish striving for human betterment?

The suicides chose their way! They wanted to ring down the curtain and end the performance that wearied them when it had just begun. "Out, out, brief candle," cries the blood-stained king. "Life's but a walking shadow,"—but these innocent, unhappy youths—the candle they blow out, and the brief shadow vanishes. This recurrent tragedy is a startling symptom. It reveals what they think of life, of their life, and its attractiveness and charm. It is indeed a dark picture. If life to them isn't worth the living, shall this not awaken churchmen to our responsibility to make it worth living? The student violence against establishment and the status quo of this hour, needs more than our pity or condemnation. This calls for spiritual revitalization and Christian consecration. We can only point the way when we are self-directed in our Christian living. The keen eyes of youth miss nothing. Whatever we do, they want to do better. When we live exclusively for pleasure, for thrills, for materials, for excitement, for selfishness, then why shouldn't they? If there is no Christ in our lives, no spiritual ideal, no holy day or holy book, or a sense of reverence, how shall they learn to put God into their lives?

I have almost forgotten the theme and the text. The story is one of the most interesting in psychology. The woman of Samaria had been psychoanalyzed by the Divine Physician. Jesus probed beneath the superficial interests in her life. He uncovered the strange mental and moral complexes of her nature. She sought to divert His interest in her personal life by bringing up superficial subjects of conversation. First, it was prejudice existing between the Jews and the Samaritans; failing in this, she turned to theology and wanted to discuss the place of worship; again, failing in this, she turned to the expectations of the coming Messiah—everything and anything to avoid her sordid personality. Christ was not victimized by her ruses. Diagnosing her need, He sent her away to a better life. Some call it psychoanalysis, while others call it conversion.

Fear, worry, and doubt are among the most destructive emotions that we experience. It is true with suicides and equally true with perverted lives. These emotions are at the root of such chronic conditions as unhappiness, nervousness, temper tantrums and lack of energy—the suicides afraid of the future and the woman at the well afraid of facts. Repressed fear comes from cowardice, resentment, stubbornness, revenge, doubt, hate, alibi, and procrastination.

Because of the thoughts we harbor and the tension that is the natural result of fear, many of our plans and ambitions go wrong and we are forced to admit failure. At this stage, the human personality has to add another destructive force to the list, *frustration*. The trinity of fear, tension, and frustration defeats our purposes. These are the drives.

Fear is a denial of God. Those of us who have called Jesus, "Lord," and who have seen the love and power of the Infinite revealed in Him, should not allow our hearts to grow fearful. It is in this way we deny Him. Fear is the failure of faith. When Martin Luther was overly wrought, his wife asked, "Is God dead?" He asked, "Why do you ask?" She answered, "Because of the way you act." In the storm on the sea of Galilee, the disciples awakened Christ and cried, "Master, carest Thou not that we perish?" He asked them, "Why are ye so fearful, how is it that ye have no faith?"When we allow fear to run riot in our lives, we are denying God. Fear is practical atheism; it matters not what our lips say. Then, we are, of all men, the most miserable and the result is incurable sadness, loneliness, and a soul destruction bent.

I once wrote in my psychology textbook: "Only the consciousness of a purpose that is mightier than any man and worthy of all men can fortify and inspirit and compose the souls of men." The author, I do not now know, but his truth I affirm. If one fears to face the future and yet remains serene and effective through all the difficulties, I am reminded of the words of a pagan philosopher, Marcus Aurelius, who wrote centuries ago: "You can always retire into yourself. There is no retreat more peaceful, less troubled, than the one a man finds within his own soul." We say, today, that all the water in the sea cannot sink a ship unless the water starts getting inside. All the trouble in the world cannot sink a man unless the trouble invades his inner life. There must be an interior castle against which the storms of life may beat without disturbing the serene quiet within.

God has prepared us to endure the storms. No matter what they are, how numerous the troubles are which attack us, we can master them. God has fitted us in advance for the victory. The coward is to be pitied, for he quits. I read that John F. Kennedy kept on his desk the motto, "This, too, shall pass." The Chicago Tribune tells of a man, unsuccessful in seeking employment, who took his own life. At the time of the funeral, a notice of a job was waiting for him in his mail box. The situation which is unendurable today, changes tomorrow. Not all changes are to the good, but sportsmanship calls for a chance. No one met with more occasional disasters than the Christ. With poise such as He demonstrated, we can gain the serenity we need, the mood that spells the difference between spiritual defeat and spiritual victory.

Serenity never comes to a person who is self-centered, who is wondering what others say about him, who is jealous of others, who is sensitive about being deprived of honor or recognition. These are the attitudes that lead to frustration and drive a man to despair and suicide. No man ever destroyed himself working for others, or in a great cause of social welfare.

Let God's quiet thoughts bring peace which the world cannot give nor take away. Naturally, I recommend worship, prayers, hymns, and the altar alone with God. I know, I have experienced it in my contacts with others. I have entered the pulpit knowing these things; and have endeavored to open inner lives to God, Whose love enfolds us all; the Father in Heaven Who banishes fear, quickens courage, lifts the mind and heart in trust. "Thou wilt keep him in perfect peace, whose mind is stayed on Thee." This is more than pious words, they can be demonstrated to every bewildered soul.

John Oxenham was the son of an important merchant in Manchester. He came to New York to represent his father's business. His life was crowded with activity. He began writing poems. I quote from "Sanctuary," written by one laboring day and night with little rest.

> " 'Mid all the traffic of the ways—
> Turmoils without, within—
> Make in my heart a quiet place,
> And come and dwell therein:
>
> A little shrine of quietness,
> All sacred to Thyself,
> Where Thou shalt all my soul possess,
> And I may find myself;
>
> A little place of mystic grace,
> Of self and sin swept bare,
> Where I may look upon Thy face,
> And talk with Thee in prayer."

THE CHURCH HAS SIGNIFICANCE

Text: "We have this treasure in earthen vessels."
—II Corinthians 4:7

Today there is a re-emphasis against insincerity. People insist upon frankness in speech as they do in candor of conduct. Our generation has become increasingly critical of the church. We admit, it is not held in the highest esteem. Yet, never in the church's history has it been without opposition. In many quarters today, it is not even in good taste to speak in support of the church. Let us be equally sincere in our analysis.

Once upon a time the church had no peer, its prominence was universally accepted. It was the guardian of science, today men turn to the laboratory; it was the mother of the arts, now they turn to the museums and art galleries; it was the healer of the sick, now they turn to the hospital; it was the founder of the drama, now they turn to the theater; it was the builder of education, now they turn to the universities. Many claim the church has ceased to function—it is a hangover from another century—the clergy buttons his collar in the back and he faces that way. Things we once considered sacred and above questioning are now fearlessly challenged. Speak ill of the church, and you are certain to get an audience.

The church is blamed for almost everything. It is too worldly or it is too otherworldly; it lacks spirituality or it fails to give social emphasis; it forgets its past or remembers only the past; it supports wars or fails in support of war in a crisis. Among church members, there is, in a measure, a defeatist attitude. In time of victory and prosperity, we say the church is arrogant. In time of difficulty and adversity, we say the church is cowardly. A paralyzing fear has taken possession of well meaning church members. They have forgotten that the world is what it is, not because of the church, but in spite of it. Let us confess that much of the criticism is justified. Those of us who love the church the most, will be the first to admit its weaknesses. We listen to the petty grievances, and if we couldn't laugh we would cry: the church lacks fellowship, the music is pitiable, the committees are chosen for favorable returns, the gossip is rampant, the preacher is mediocre, the services are too long. The list is too long and too familiar to elaborate. On the average Sunday, we can hear, "The ritual is too ancient and meaningless," or "The ritual is not emphasized and is gone over hurriedly." Some say, "The sermons are too long," and after the same sermons another contends, "We can't pay his salary for a ten minute pep talk."

I will admit, the church needs overhauling and must rid itself of much of the ecclesiastical machinery, the empty ceremonies, and idle words. With adequate budgets, in most cases, and council meetings, it is giving only limited service in time and talent where it is needed. In spite of these confessed weaknesses, the church has been strong enough to plant religion even in the soil of Caesar and amid the opposition of Hitler and Stalin. It has gone to every frontier and kindled hope in the hearts of the pioneers. It has developed some men who could live kindly and morally in the midst of vulgarity, extreme cruelty, and vice. In the words of old Dr. Glover, "The Christians have outthought, outlived, and outdied the people around them." We know that in spite of church bigotry and narrowness, we cannot picture a worthwhile institution, agency, or organization that has not had its origin in the church. Today, when there is a need, the people turn to the church for benevolences. It is a treasure in an earthen vessel.

Back of every church movement, there is a high desire to uplift mankind, redeem womanhood, and preserve childhood. No other institution is doing this. John Kennedy said, "It is not what the country can do for you, it is what you can do for your country." It is what we can do for the church—if wrong, reform it! Grafters and chiselers in government and unions do not stop them from their functions and their reason for being. The greater the faults, the greater must be reform efforts. Perhaps there are some in the church who ought to be out, but there are definitely some out who ought to be in. Christians are "living epistles, known and read of men." The difficulty I find in the church, is a group of well-meaning anemic people who haven't taken Christ seriously. They have never been challenged with REAL CHRISTIANITY. There is no rich quality about their lives to attract others, no revealing of Christ. There is no manifestation of what the church offers or why it exists. The professions are noble, the deeds are few. It must be said, the faults are greater because we expect greater things from the church. We can judge the church, as we do all other organizations, by its enemies as well as by its friends.

What is significant about the church? First, I would say its heritage. We join hands with an ageless fellowship of which we may be proud. Think of the changes wrought in the men who walked with the Christ. A variety of natures made up that little band, and each unfolded in his own way. Out of poor material, Christ built world leaders. The church, today, is upheld by the same power that first brought it into being. Christ took an impetuous, impulsive, unstable fisherman and called him a rock. Time justified His judgment. Here was an earthen vessel with a heavenly treasure. I believe Emerson is eternally right when he says, "What is necessary abides, in the long run only what is real endures." Let us remember that churches come and go, but the CHURCH UNIVERSAL goes on forever. The church endures because the builders founded it upon the needs of humanity, and if, by some vast catastrophe, it were destroyed tomorrow it would be rebuilt in some form by the same principles that brought it into being. The twelve had something take hold of them that was undying; and they knew if they witnessed to its power, it would take hold of others and endure. They went against every form of opposition to preach the kingdom of brotherhood, peace, good will, and righteousness. They were jailed, but they were free; outcast, but they had a home of the soul undefiled; hated, but they loved their Gospel and knew that love conquers men and nations. They preached "The Cross— by this sign conquer."

What is significant about the church? It enables men to reappraise themselves in a world where things are in the saddle, in a time of automation, geared up efficiency, mass production, jet propulsion, and rapid transit. The business goal is not to produce to satisfy demands, but rather to create new wants to consume what the machine produces. The greatest effort apparently is in advertising. We are existing in wheels, speed, competition, and mobility—only the church cares for the soul. "Be still, and know that I am God." The Sabbath of meditation, if we use it, is medicine that heals and saves. "The things which are seen are temporal, but the things which are not seen are eternal." The church asks that we remember enduring values that build day by day and build for all eternity. What can be more significant than true values incorporated into character?

This religion in the church is not a luxury, it is a necessity. It is the cement of society; and it behooves those of us who hold the treasure, the hard-won inheritance, to renew our vows at the altar. It is not an accident that the anarchy of our day is atheistic, for it has been born in crass materialism. Religion today must be defined in terms of duty and activity—to use Immanuel Kant's definition, "The recognition of all our duties as divine commands." This is the categorical imperative. We have seen when moral ideals grow dim, humanity becomes a mob and men march in violence to overthrow establishment.

What is the significance of the church? It repossesses self. It brings the secular mind into moral conformity. It pulls self together and unites split personalities. We work at the loom six days a week; on Sunday, in church, we get back of the moving looms to readjust the failures and the possibility of neglecting to look at the pattern we are weaving. The church must offer more than ethics. The church offers a mountain top experience where we get a clearer, broader, higher, view of what is and what ought to be. "It sees life steadily and sees it whole." It brings celestial light when darkened with routine mundane things. The church says, "He restoreth my soul." Only the church has this *spiritual concern.*

The church, then, is a living, creative, conserving, redeeming fellowship; a comradeship, not commandments; a fellowship, not philosophy; it satisfies the heart hunger of men; it is at once a community and a communion. If we are to conserve it, we must improve it, adapting it to the needs and issues of the age, following the ways of the spirit leading us from faith to faith. The significance of the church is to give reverence, an atmosphere of God's presence. It is to be the Kingdom of God, not the kingdom of men. It declares that socialism may humanize life, and education rationalize it, and business mechanize it, but the church has one and only one mission and that is to spiritualize life. Social justice alone is not what it seeks, it preaches divine justice. The church is not man-centered, it is God-centered. We must remember we can have religion without being religious. The church does not distribute wealth but practices stewardship. It begins in the old Jerusalem, but it ends only in the new Jerusalem—born in time but ending in eternity. It holds high the throne of God to keep the world sane.

In the church, we learn the unity of spirit in the fellowship of worship, the secret of power, and the bonds of peace. When we argue, we are divided; when we sing, we are one. In the home of my professor of systematic theology, Dr. Cleland B. McAfee, on Sunday afternoons, he would play this hymn of his own composition. We would sing:

"There is a place of quiet rest—
Near to the heart of God,
A place where sin cannot molest—
Near to the heart of God.

There is a place of full release—
Near to the heart of God,
A place where all is joy and peace—
Near to the heart of God.

O Jesus, blest Redeemer—
Sent from the heart of God,
Hold us who wait before Thee—
Near to the heart of God."

The church of significance will be a place of hearing, wherein, if we listen together, we shall hear that still small voice, which will be audible for such as have ears to hear—when all the confusions of today have followed the feet that made them into silence. In the heights, as in the depths, the church is one eternal, unconquerable treasure in an earthen vessel.

THE LAW OF PROGRESS

Proverbs 14:34–"Righteousness exalteth a nation."

The primary duty of a college is to train students so they will enter the world unafraid and with constructive purposes and skills. With these educational privileges, the mission is to shape ideas and ideals and contribute to society something wholesome and constructive. Today, I wish to show that world progress never moves in a straight line, nor on an even grade. We will see the ebb and flow, the rise and fall, the swing to the right, then to the left. I hope to show the result that is gained in the degree to which morals are the criterion, and the maintenance of righteousness is upheld and advanced. Your individual career will have similar irregularities. We will see how man reacts to good and evil; and, consequently, how he progresses and retrogresses.

Let us begin by making a simple statement; the principle of progress and retardation will be clearer in our thinking. There is an elementary truth of physics, that if anything is to fall, it must first rise up; action brings reaction; a man cannot fall lying flat on the ground. This is more than physics in human relations, it is the history of life. A society of savages cannot suffer decadence or decay, any more than animals can be moral or immoral. They are governed by instinct. So long as man remained a savage, he definitely followed the tribal routine. He knew neither renaissance nor reformation; but, with elevation came the peril of a fall–the higher the ascent, the more disastrous the collapse. The privilege of growth involves the glory but also the danger. This is the paradox of morals, the tragic element in history, the substance of the stern admonitions spoken to the present out of the past.

The largest, most fascinating, and significant fact within

the range of man's mind is the movement of human society across the fields of past centuries. History enables us to observe this movement for some eight thousand years. Beyond this, all we know is by inference and guess. Here is man, hidden away in the depths of primeval forests, or roaming the great plains of the various continents. He possesses few tools and weapons. He is in competition with nature and the beasts of the fields and forests. He is without art, literature, industry, and has only tribal rules of government. His life is constant warfare. Apart from the Genesis story, he is a wholly incomplete individual. He lives by hunting and eating the spontaneous products of the earth. He is not moral or immoral for he, too, follows the law of survival of the fittest and the struggle for existence. He knows no right or wrong.

If we return to the law of rudimentary physics we know that if a body falls, it falls down, never up. This is equally true of early man, although this is one of man's oldest delusions, and he attempts to deny it. Philosophically he says that grossness is greatness and that decline is an ascent. This is a sad deception! We do not fall up—we have to climb up. If we prefer appearance to reality, veneer to substance, quantity to quality, cheapness to value, counterfeit to genuineness—then we may be sure that our direction is downward and will end in havoc. Everything lifted tends to fall. Nature counts it unsafe to permit any wrong to go unpunished: fire burns, acids eat, rocks crush, steam scalds, just as iron rusts, wood rots and marble disintegrates. It takes effort to keep things on high. Human institutions tend to fall. The moral effort is too costly for weaklings, and the struggle is abandoned. A large part of history is the tragedy of ruins: ruined empires, ruined religions, ruined philosophies, ruined liberty, ruined souls. This is our major concern: to analyze and discern why and how the great works of man end in grievous failure; why institutions, after enduring opposition and overcoming every form of difficulty, should lose power to survive and overcome. When we have learned to live, why do we lose the power to outlive? Why, after displaying mighty strength, do we end in miserable weakness?

Man cleared the forests, populated the plains, organized society, and built governments for orderly conduct and harmony. He refined his culture to an art. The distance between the primitive and the refinement of society we call human progress. We say that the human race has moved onward and upward. The poet says: "Civilization is a tree that is nourished, not by rain and snow, but by tears and blood." The life of the higher rests upon the death of the lower. The lack of incentives and right impulses has reverted the process, and the higher has been sacrificed for the lower. Hosea contended that the national collapse came when the moral teachers were not heard; and without vision, the people perished. There was no man to climb the mountain top to commune with the invisible and then descend with a message. The vision splendid had died in the light of the common day.

The way of neglect of the basic truths in morals shows the wreckage of races and people and nations. Institutions and philosophies have waxed strong and fallen. The past, contrary to the evolutionist, has not always been onward and upward forever. We have evolution but also devolution; we have left behind collapsed civilizations. Hopes and aspirations furnished the springs of survival. Man had to declare that the dead past must bury its dead. The future belonged to those who would correct past errors. Resurrection follows the death and gives hope of recovery. There is a power, some condition, some element, which enables institutions and agencies to survive while others fall and perish As students, we are to inquire into the conditions of human improvements and to discover the reason for the impulses that enable the social structure of mankind to endure and move upward.

These questions have always engaged reflecting minds, but never more deeply or more anxiously than in this period of history. In our troubled world, with its unsettlement; and when the foundations are shaken; and when the political, social, and moral formulas are under judgment, we need a re-examination of our systems. What are the causes, what are the symptoms of decay? In our review of the rise and fall of civilizations, I question if we can make definite answer. Generalization of principles will not suffice. We have to proceed inductively, and we do this by citing examples of downfalls, and then drawing from them the conclusions that they warrant. Our first example will be the prodigious collapse of the classic world, the fall of the Roman empire.

The Roman, or more accurately the Romanized, world did not decay from lack of intelligence, as we understand it today. In this assembly, I believe I am safe in believing that you would contend that mankind has progressed because of increasing intellectuality, and that the supreme, functioning power in human progress is the mind of man. We emphasize our increased mental powers. We have, by the inherent potencies of a new intellectuality, mastered the environment and discovered the secret of knowledge; hence, humanity has advanced. Men are coming to idolize intellect. Brilliance is placed before goodness and intellectual dexterity above fidelity. Intellect walks the earth a crowned king, while morality is enslaved, as custom practiced.

The Roman emperors, from Augustus to Constantine, and even farther, from Constantine to Justinian, counted among them a high proportion of able and active men. Few dynasties of equal duration can show a higher proportion. They had for guidance an incomparable experience in war and jurisprudence, and were ingenious in the conduct of foreign affairs. They built up an elaborate system of domestic and colonial government and extended citizenship ever more widely. When the empire became too great for one-man rule, they brought in a co-emperorship and reformed the army; they drew up codifications of law. In nearly all the activities of managing a state they were industrious, resourceful, and open to experiment.

Now, examine what they failed to do. While great schemes in political management were being invented, the population of Rome was ignored. With the disappearance of free agriculture and small holdings, thousands of people had swarmed into the capital. They were idle, consequently dangerous, and constituted a problem that was basically moral and political. No question was so important to the fate of the empire as whether the problem was moral or political. Unfortunately, it was treated as purely political, and was altogether ignored as moral. The experienced men who governed, so wise to their age, so stupid to all succeeding ages, looked upon that mass of idlers as merely a mob that had to be maneuvered into safety. The wise governors fed them free; next, they provided amusement for them, again at the cost of the state. On three days a week, there were games in the circus, perhaps as often there were plays in the theater. The circus games consisted chiefly of fights between wild beasts, fights between wild beasts and men, and fights unto death of men with one another.

In the theater the spectacles became more and more obscene and more and more cruel. Often a duel on the stage was a real duel, ending in death, so demanded by the audience. In these ways, hundreds of thousands of people were saturated with brutality and obsessed with lust. It was one long perversion, one continued abnormality, one persistent moral and mental aberration. This is what was given to the population of the chief city of the world in order to make them forget that they had lost their liberty; forget that they once had a country which offered them a spiritual ideal. Concurrently they had lost their souls. The sagacious governors did not see that ruin was inevitable. They were theorists and practitioners of politics. They were realists calling for facts, for efficiency, that today we would call pragmatism. They could see militarism and its science, the usefulness of regimentation, the value of a cavalry, and of all the power instruments of destruction, but they could not see moral infection that inevitably brings annihilation. The public spirit gone, religion dying, morals in decay, and yet they knew everything except what was worth knowing.

In Greece, 2400 to 2700 years ago, the intellect was so remarkable that they produced things which lie at the summit of mental ability. In art, in all of its forms, in architecture, in oratory, spoken and written, in poetry, in drama, and in history, they united their forces and idolized intellect. Intellect was upon their throne; thinkers, the architects of their civilization. Their god was simply an infinite brain, an eternal logic machine, cold as steel, weaving endless ideas about life and art, about nature and man. Greece reached the highest altitude of any nation in history. It was not only true of the elect but of the common people. At their Olympian games, the citizenship gathered their literary productions that now we read; their art was exhibited to the delight of the people; music was rendered which the common man of the street, in our twentieth century, could not appreciate. If the element of progress, of social stability, be intellectual capacity–then the civilization of Greece should have endured. It, too, is gone. They eliminated themselves entirely from the unequivocal law of survival. The springs of civilization are not in the mind, but in the heart of morals.

The element of progress, the condition of stability, is not pure intellectuality. Greece, like Rome, refutes the assumption. I say this to a college graduating class, and, I beg of you, continue your studies. Nevertheless, reflect how often the clever are of incredible stupidity and the learned of incredible obtuseness. Face facts! Cleverness and learning are merely sharpening of wits, as a mere filling up of the mind as one fills a bag. We have many blotter minds, perhaps carrying a "key,"–minds with utter decadence, ineptitude and rottenness. Decadent culture has had more to do with bringing disaster upon mankind than mere illiteracy ever had. When the illiterate have destroyed great institutions or ideals, they have been led usually by the clever, who have first destroyed the soul of man. Mark well: I do not scoff at knowledge; knowledge is power. The world listens to the man who knows. Francis Bacon's dictum is still true, "Reading maketh a full man, conference a ready man and writing an exact man." The old Arabic proverb said that understanding is the wealth of wealth. How noble Bacon's aphorism! How petty his envy and avarice! What scholarship he had and what cunning! He advanced arguments for liberty and free education, yet exercised meanness and accepted bribes from the rich against the poor; he starved his reputation, but more importantly, his soul. For centuries, the work of moralists has been not so much the making known of new truth as inspiring men to do a truth already known.

When the tumult and shouting dies and conventionalities have vanished, there remains rooted in the solid center of existence, the truth: *Man is Soul!* If this is forgotten or scorned by dynasties or democracies, by the stately or the learned, then one thing is certain, retribution draws near. Wise Solomon stood and watched his city perish. Great was Goethe's genius, yet self-indulgence took his friends' time to keep his reputation alive. The stories of Byron, Shelley, Poe, and others of great intellect reveal vice poisoning their genius. Milton said he had first to teach the lessons of character by incorporating their principles. It was not a scholar, in the proper sense of the word, but a politician, Theodore Roosevelt, who said, "To educate a man in mind and not in morals is to educate a menace to society." Lincoln, in matured judgment, said: "I am not bound to win, but I am bound to be true. I am not bound to succeed but I am bound to live up to the light I have."

The medieval world saw the most successful effort ever made to unite a continent. There was one infallible, unimpeachable, incontrovertible, authentic church for all mankind. The head of the church was "papa." The church and papacy constituted one supreme international, religious tribunal; with one language, Latin; one standard of conduct and education; one inerrant absolute. At its word, armies moved. Here was power, ability, wealth, that surpassed ancient Rome; it drew information from every corner of the globe. Everything that signified invincible strength, it had. If anything in the world promised indefinite duration, it was this theocratic institution with absolute polity. Again, today, we read of the dissolution.

.The fall came because moral souls were eternal in their varieties, pure in conscience, and clear of purpose. They could no longer endure the lust for wealth, the false pronouncements of power over the things of earth and heaven. Savonarola, Wycliffe, Huss, Luther, Melanchthon, Zwingli, Calvin, Knox, and many others, cried for reform. They protested and became protestant reformers. These voices thundered for morality and spiritual guidance. Purity, decency, decorum, virtue, and sobriety, alone could endure. Righteousness exalts not only a nation, but a church; sin is a reproach. When restraints have been obliterated, disciplines banished, moral judgments cast aside, and we obey impulses, then death is inevitable. We have substituted the burning of candles, repeating prayers, singing hymns, chanting creeds, exercising religion, and we have lost our souls. The reformation should not end. We must begin with morals to have a religion. We cannot have religion without morals any more than an enduring state or civilization without morals.

The eternal never left Himself without witnesses and never will. There will always be prophets' warnings to offer inspiration needed in any recovery. Listen to Paul who spoke of obscenity, impurity, degradation, cruelty, indolence, and corrupt luxury; hear him pronounce judgment. He offered the solution by preaching One Who could evoke that loyalty and inspire obedience, a voice of power, a life contagious with energy, the One Whose Gospel of the Kingdom was the solid substance of existence. His enthusiasm showed the prosaic or matter of fact basis upon which rests the fulfillment of souls. He had in His wings the healing of nations. We can understand why Matthew Arnold contended that conduct is three-fourths of life. The Christ commanded us to hunger and thirst after righteousness. The end of life is the crown of righteousness. This is the secret of history. *This alone is the law of progress,* not intellectuality, art, science, but *morality.* In Amos 5:24 we read: "Let justice roll down as waters and righteousness as a mighty stream."

This is the inviolable law we find in the stories of Babylon, Egypt, Persia, Phoenicia, Syria, Greece, Rome, Spain, and the others. Can America endure? We, too, are clever with power, shrewd manipulators, and masters of the material arts. Let us declare categorically: "We can win the world and lose our souls." Bear in mind, history is a perpetual day of judgment. I have said many times, in many places, that freedom is independence from unjust restraint, but *not independence from properly constituted authority.* It means only that we are free to do what is right; and we are not to confuse liberty with license, nor freedom with irresponsibility, nor human rights with their perversions. It is not being quick of tongue, but profound of soul. Nations disintegrate because men are corrupt. The omnipotent and omniscient God has put us under the law and we must obey or suffer the consequences. We are punished *by* our sins. The law is moral. It is eternal righteousness. It is the law of progress.

You leave the lecture halls to get gold. I wish you every success but remember gold must be spiritualized; you seek property that, too, must be consecrated; you seek results, but in gaining, unite them with modesty; you strive for social position, but unite that with humility; in all your getting, the final good is in service. You have been here with others to get and then to give. I have on my desk a Greek aphorism I would leave with you: "So act as to elicit the best in others and thereby in one's self." Between us and the fulfillment of the desires expressed, rise mountains of war, of unfair dealings, of national selfishness, of international insincerities, and class divisions. Righteousness, alone, will remove these mountains for they disappear not by faith in treaties that turn to scraps of paper, nor by faith in dictators, in ammunition, in trade compacts, but by morality.

Without the ethical principles which have built nations, the ancient prophets would say: "It is so easy to talk morals but so difficult to live with them." Remember, no reform comes easily. We must listen to Him Who drew lessons deeper than the schools have ever learned, and set on high the ideal by which we shall endure. Leave Him and we are impoverished. He has the language for the ages. He has taught us that salvation of the temporal is only in the eternal and that the fulfillment of mortality is in the immortal. Confronted as we are by the ruins and glories of history, both vindicating the presence of God among men, what will our decision be?

> "Great roads the Romans built that men might meet,
> And walls to keep strong men apart—secure.
> Now centuries have gone, and in defeat
> The walls are fallen, but the roads endure."
> —E. M. Hartwich

A NEW COMMANDMENT FOR THE OLD WORLD

Text: "A new commandment I give you, that ye love one
another, even as I have loved you."
—John 13:34

Christianity has many aspects and may be described
under many forms, but it approaches the whole truth in our
text, "to love one another." This is God's attempt to love the
world into goodness. In Jesus Christ, the Eternal Father has
generated and shed forth the powers of love, entrusting the
hope of recovering the world to Himself to the operations of
this supreme passion.

Christianity is the religion of love. That is easily said but
the dimensions of this simple but stupendous affirmation
have never been comprehended by man. All of Jesus' life falls
into three exhaustive categories. He said something—He was a
teacher. He did something—He lived the life of man. He
died—and His death was so sublime that the instrument of
torture has become the most sacred sign of mankind. As a
teacher, He added nothing to natural science, politics,
economics, or jurisprudence. His contribution enriched ethics
beyond compare. Intellectually, His supreme contribution
was the discovery of LOVE. He called the omnipotent Spirit,
"Father." The greatest and most fertile thought ever projected into or received by the mind of man was born.

Let us endeavor to see Christ as His contemporaries saw
Him. He entered the world of the scribes and Pharisees
preaching "Love." Their God, Jehovah, was localized that He
might be monopolized. The rabbinical school subsidized their
learning to the exclusive caste. It was a world of ultra-
orthodoxy. Without criticism and giving only analysis, we
would say it was contemptuous and supercilious; with var-
iance, enmity, hostility and malice. In the "days of His

113

flesh," this was the environment in which He had His being.
When He struggled against it, lived contrary to it, and
attempted to correct it, he was a radical, a heretic, a traitor,
and an innovator to be murdered.

His critics cried, "He is a friend of publicans and
sinners." It is true, He was not only contending for kindness,
charity, philanthropy, and tolerance, but above all these
ethical expressions, He was preaching *brotherhood*. To be a
friend of a publican, Samaritan, sinner, was unthinkable. The
publicans were tax-collectors, taking money from their own
people and paying tribute to the oppressor of the Jews. Over
and above the tax, came their loot; it was authorized
plundering. The synagogue refused their tithes, prohibited
them from the temple, and completely rejected their testimonies in court. They were religious outcasts and social
dregs. Jesus not only ate with them, but elected one,
Matthew, to be His disciple. When Theodore Roosevelt spoke
to the colored outside the White House, that was endured;
but to have them eat in the White House brought general
indignation. Christ said the publicans were members of God's
family and brothers under a heavenly Father. He ate with
them.

Christ showed no preference, whether men were good or
bad, rich or poor, literate or illiterate, religious or irreligious.
He recognized no race, color, class, nationality, or creed. A
man was "a man for a' that." He healed the sick, fed the
hungry, praised sacrificial service, comforted the sorrowful,
forgave Zacchaeus the rich, preached to Nicodemus the
scholar, and enjoyed home hospitality of Mary and Martha.
The Rabbis couldn't stifle Him; the Pharisees could not
terrify Him; the ritualists could not misguide Him; and the
nationalists could not dwarf Him. In the midst of hatred, He
loved. Surrounded by Levitical laws, He used universal
principles; in a traditional atmosphere where the past was
reverenced, He spoke of progress and the coming of the
Kingdom. In extreme nationalism and creed observances, He

spoke of the good Samaritan, a hated race and religion. In the midst of warring sects, He was thoroughly catholic. He spoke of the peacemakers as the children of God. He was building the Kingdom of righteousness in the souls of men, and not on the hills of Judea. It was to be a Kingdom of the physician, the teacher, the preacher, the returning prodigal, the child, and the forgiving Father.

Read the message of the Christ, and see how carefully He was clearing away obstacles and dissipating clouds which concealed the graciousness of God. In sermon and parable, He interpreted His own life and man's relation to God in terms of LOVE. He made God loveable. This is the central truth and the new commandment, "that ye love one another, as I have loved you." His theology is summarized, "God is Love." His ethics are summarized, "Love one another." He was not a theorist; He proposed no scheme of social adjustment, commended neither democracy nor communism, set forth no code of corrective law. He told men to love. He believed in love—believed that it dissipates all bitter and unholy tempers, expels all envy, avarice, and hardheartedness. He praised mercy and commanded forgiveness and brotherly love. A Christian, before anything else, is in harmony with his fellows.

The last night of Christ's earthly life, when the shadow of the Cross was thrown upon His path, and the last commission was to be given, He said to the disciples, "Love one another." He did not speak as a teacher, this was over; He spoke like a father; He called them, "little children." Tradition tells us that St. Jerome wrote that the beloved John, old and too feeble to walk, was carried into the Ephesus Church. Seated in a chair, he said, "Little children, love one another." This is the Gospel's crowning proof that we belong to Christ. This is not a suggestion, it is a commandment—a law that cannot be ignored.

Strange it is, how theologians and preachers have ignored this command! It is not in our creeds. Love and the

Kingdom were the central themes of Christ, but not of our doctrines. We are too ecclesiastical, with forms, rituals, ceremonies, sacraments, polity, and traditions. If we have the spirit of Christ, we have everything; if we fail in this, we have nothing. A man may be baptized with water, but if he is not baptized of the spirit, he is none of His. He may take the communion elements, but if he lacks the spirit he is none of His. He may repeat every creed of the historic church, but if he has not the spirit of the Christ, he is none of His. This is not a dictum, but a truth. We can speak with the tongues of men and of angels, but if we have not love, we are clanging cymbals. We can have faith that removes mountains, a faith once delivered unto the saints, but if we have not love, we are none of His. We can have all the logic, rationalism, and knowledge, but have not love, then we have nothing. We can give our bodies to be burned, give all our goods to feed the poor, but if we lack love, it profiteth nothing. Philanthropy is not religion. It is possible to give, do it to advertise, and at the same time have enmity in our hearts. Martyrs are plentiful and often fanatical, superstitious, and ignorant, even if they are absolutely sincere.

Christ loved; He was all sympathy, human woe moved Him. He carried all griefs, He felt all pains. A college professor, asking questions, kept Him awake far into the night. A woman's sin made Him forget to eat. The faces of children opened His arms to embrace. He heard the cry of the beggar above the pressing crowd; felt the touch of faith in the thronged street; was broken hearted over an impenitent city; pitied the breadless multitude; wept with the mourning sisters, and ended by saying, "I lay down My life for My sheep." This is humanity's holiest love story.

Friendship is cardinal and indispensable. In religion, worship follows brotherliness. "Go, be reconciled to thy brother, then come and worship." "He that loveth not his brother whom he hath seen, cannot love God Whom he hath not seen." Church bigots, ecclesiastical autocrats, have no part of Christ. The Kingdom He preached is swayed by love. The reason the Kingdom is not here is because the church itself has not demonstrated the unselfishness, the unity, and harmony that Christ illustrated and preached. A divided church is a stumbling block and cannot be a church because it is not Chrisitan. "By this men will know ye are My disciples, if you love one another." It is not the shining of the mind, nor mere righteousness, the rectified conscience, the ethical will, that bring salvation, it is LOVE. This is the Christly virtue, the issues of life are heart issues. The world has stoned harlots from the beginning, but there is never a harlot less. The harlot, Magdalene, was loved into the Kingdom of purity. The best elements in life, the noblest impulses, and purest deeds are born in Christian love. Our difficulty lies in the fact that we have pagan hearts trying to worship in Christian temples. The church may have money and members, but can be poverty stricken in LOVE. The virulence and bitterness of doctrinal controversies among so-called Christians prove that churches are untouched by His spirit.

When we surrender love, no other truth is worth having. I am not contending for uniformity in doctrine and polity, but I am declaring: "To be Christian we must have the unity of spirit in the bond of peace." We need a united church in this divided world. It is a world calling for Christ. We need to cast out demons called suspicion, hatred, revenge. God works to cure earth's sin and sorrow. The discords of sin and grief will pass when we heed the command, "Love one another, as I have loved you." "Every one that loveth is born of God."

> "A mightier Church shall come, whose convenant word
> Shall be the deeds of love. Not 'Credo.' Then—
> 'Amo' shall be the password through the gates.
> Man shall not ask his brother any more,
> 'Believeth thou?' but 'Loveth thou?' And all
> Shall answer at God's altar, 'Lord, I love.'
> For Hope may anchor, Faith may steer, but Love,
> Great Love alone, is captain of the soul."

> —Henry B. Carpenter

MORE THINGS ARE WROUGHT BY PRAYER

Text: "He ever liveth to make intercession for us."
—Hebrews 7:25

The tragedy of "Hamlet" is recognized to be the acme of Shakespeare's genius. Hamlet, himself, after he has received the terrifying disclosures from the ghost upon the platform at Elsinore, dismisses his friend, Horatio, with these words, "For my own poor part, look you, I'll go pray." In this imaginative literature, we find in the character of Hamlet a portrayal of a type known to all men in all places. Hamlet is pictured under strain, surrounded by dark situations, a man who has suffered loss, a man who is called to grave responsibilities. He is one of those poor, burdened, distressed lives so common in our world.

The plot is familiar to all of us: Hamlet grieved over losing his father whom he fondly loved; the injustice of having the crown wrested from his own head by his uncle; the discovery of the treachery of that murderous uncle, and darker and heavier than all else, his own mother's participation in the crime and her indecent haste to enter into an incestuous union with the murderer; the knowledge that all around him the court was one mass of deep-lying intrigue and falsity. Such is the situation of the man, Hamlet, and it is at this point that we hear him saying to Horatio, "For my own part, look you, I'll go pray." A burdened man, flèeing to the secret chamber of prayer, a distressed, grieved, broken life, charged with awful responsibilities, going into solitude; he goes to find strength beyond himself.

William James, in his renowned volume, "The Varieties of Religious Experience," tells of a discussion about the efficacy of prayer. Many reasons are given why we should NOT pray; others why we SHOULD pray; very little is said about why we DO pray. The reason is simple: we cannot refrain from praying. This, of course, is an analysis from psychology and the human mind. The same conclusion could come from anthropology and the study of human history. All men pray! They have always prayed, not that they have been taught, or commanded, but because "Man is made that way."

In front of the Museum of Fine Arts in Boston, is a striking equestrian statue of an Indian. With outstretched arms, he is seated on a horse, head aloft, eyes looking to the heavens. No one has taught him to pray. The Greek word for man is "anthropos," meaning "the upward looking one." Man is the only animal that is born to look up, from whence comes his help. His own heart and instinct have given him this nature and aptitude. The Arab with his prayer-rug in the desert, prays at the rising and the setting of the sun. Theology simply says that it is man's sense of dependence. Philosophy says it is *agitur sequitur esse,* "Our actions flow from our nature." Birds fly, fish swim, dogs run, man prays. Why? It is nature.

Prayer rises from the chronic state of dependence in the cosmos. Man is surrounded by these great natural resources that appeal to him as mysterious and inescapable. His life is beset by perils from the existence of nature, the elements in heaven and on earth, and wild beasts around about. He cannot live a self-contained life, he must appeal to forces greater than his own. As we look across the field of humanity, as far back as the eye can reach, we find poor, distressed, pained humanity at prayer. Prayer is the universal fact of history, seeking help in prayer, asking unseen power in the universe to rescue and redeem.

There are many definitions of prayer. It is a symptom. Prayer is an indication of that deep disease which lies at the heart of man's being, the disease of doubt and fear, the disease of sin. Wherever man flees to the chamber of prayer and lifts his hands upward seeking the divine, it is because he is distressed, he is after help, and is in search of power to enable him to meet the responsibilities of life. He needs courage in the face of danger.

In my study I have a radio and a television set. I realize that if I turn a dial I can both hear and see that there are vast reservoirs of energy, if I make adjustment to them. Like all electrical gadgets, we do not know where the power resides, but we know that we live and move and have our being in its presence. Man has harnessed the power by tapping the reservoir and using it for his welfare. Why not the use of the Divine Power that is available, the infinite something we call God? When we pray, we are lifting up our mystical needs to the unsearchable reservoir of divine wisdom, comfort, and strength, whereby we may receive for ourselves the help which we need. In the words of St. Augustine, "Thou hast made us for Thyself, O God, and our hearts are restless until they find rest in Thee." Nothing absolutely nothing, can stop the human heart in this quest.

The difficulty we find in prayer is our concept of moving Divine Will and making it subservient to the human will. We have said that all men pray, but we do not say they pray wisely. They do not pray to the heavenly Father which Christ taught. They have often prayed to the planets, to animals, to human leaders. Remember, Kipling writes: "who makes his prayer to a rag, a bone, a hank of hair." Men have made gods of women. The northwest Indians used to speak of Mt. Rainier as "the mountain that was god." In fact, we have had men like Alexander the Great, Napoleon, Hitler, and Japanese emperors who have considered themselves gods.

A man says, "I asked God to save my baby's life and my prayer was not answered." A man may pray for rain, to him it would be a blessing, but the same rain might be a hardship on his neighbor. In war, we have the two contending forces praying to the same God. Both say they are on God's side, and the fact is, God is not on either side. It has been said that to pray for a tiny stone to be moved one yard up the shore, would change the history of the world. It would require stronger winds and waves, a stronger pull of the moon, a heavier gale, which would change the temperature, which would change the temperament of the people, which would change the history of the world. The Divine Will is already perfect, and we cannot expect to alter it. It is the will of perfect wisdom, of perfect love, of absolute goodness; therefore, we cannot attempt to vary divine decrees. One of the finest prayers in the Bible was uttered by the boy, Samuel,—only six words, "Speak, Lord, for Thy servant heareth."

Prayer is not an attempt to guide God, but to let God guide us. It has been said that prayer is so great a power that by it we can "move the hands that move the universe." Our prayers so often sound like an attempt to win God over to our point of view, to obtain His support in something that we want to do, to plead with Him to intervene on our behalf in some struggle that is becoming too hard for us. It is our duty to place ourselves humbly and trustfully into the hands of God, that we ourselves may be moved by Him toward that which is His will for us.

Many of us believe that prayer means, not the power to change the Divine Will, but in the power, to open the choked channels which lie between God and the spirit of man. There is in man's nature a capacity to receive power from the unseen spirit of God, but the infinite resources must be kept open and active. I believe that prayer is simply the soul putting itself into an attitude of receptivity, breaking down the hindrances on the part of man, against the approach of the beneficent power of God.

This law of free flow is older than Christianity in its application. The wisest of the intellectual Greeks used it. Socrates prayed many times for hours on end. The orator, Demosthenes, whose eloquence was unequaled, began his lectures with prayer. Pericles, the leader of the Athenian state, at every crisis, prayed. Epictetus, Seneca, and the pagan philosopher, Marcus Aurelius, before every commitment to the people, went into the sacred chamber for meditation, we call prayer. They knew, and we know, that meditation, or prayer, is not reaching for things beyond our reach. Prayer is a tremendous search for personal power. It is the means of the fulfillment of the divine possibilities which lie within the mystical potentialities of man's nature. This has been true down through the centuries.

Why should twentieth century man pray? Christ prayed, can we do less? He prayed at the baptism which was His initial act of self-consecration, offering Himself to God. He prayed all night before He chose the disciples—presumably for light and guidance. He prayed at the transfiguration, offering Himself to God for men. He prayed in Gethsemane, "Let this cup pass,"—the only time He prayed for respite, but the prayer ends, "Thy will be done." On the Cross, He prayed twice—once for those who crucified Him and when He offered His spirit in death, unto God. He asked time and again only for God. He asked nothing for Himself, neither refuge nor comfort. His prayer was to do the Father's will.

Herein we have disclosed the trouble with the world. It has been our will against the will of God. The spiritual energies of our lives are flagging; we lack spiritual vitality; there is a drooping. The cause is spiritual depletion, the want of energizing. We have spent ourselves without recharging the spiritual batteries. We are consequently dissatisfied, weak, and irritated, in a state of restlessness. Youth, today, has not learned the meaning of spiritual vitality. They have turned to the use of drugs, which is one of the greatest evils of youth in all ages. We poor men, women, and children of the twentieth century, with all our wealth, technology, science, wisdom, and everything that our great age has poured upon us, are an unhappy and dissatisfied lot.

Our need is for spiritual refreshment. We are dropping the habit of prayer. We have abandoned meditation for the "noise of selfish strife," and we have not been able to hear His voice telling us to "Be still and know that I am God." We have lost the art of detachment. We never uncover the soul to infinite powers. The nature of man can no more live apart from God, than the seed can live apart from light, heat, and moisture.

The great things of life come to us in our solitudes. In the lines of John Greenleaf Whittier:

> "Drop Thy still dews of quietness,
> Till all our strivings cease;
> Take from our souls the strain and stress,
> And let our ordered lives confess
> The beauty of Thy peace."

Take our sorrows: when our hearts are in review before the world we set our faces in rigidity and refuse to drop a tear; in the lone hour apart, there comes the upwelling of that chastened sorrow which we have concealed from the world. Poor, needy, failing, burdened, strained men and women, with the responsibilities and exactions of life upon us, we need to go down into the quiet, hushed places, into the hour of solitude, and there, uncovering our souls to the infinite environment of love and of wisdom and of guidance and of comfort, simply ask that we be strengthened. Landor writes, "Solitude is the audience-chamber of God." "For my own poor part, look you, Horatio, I'll go pray." Alfred Tennyson wrote:

> "More things are wrought by prayer
> Than this world dreams of. . . . .
> For what are men better than sheep or goats
> That nourish a blind life within the brain,
> If, knowing God, they lift not hands of prayer
> Both for themselves and those who call them friends?
> For so the whole round earth is every way
> Bound by gold chains about the feet of God."

MR. WILLIAM STUHR

In Memoriam

The building of the temple was one of the important events during the reign of the kings. It was work for expert craftsmen—first the architect with his gift of vision for beauty and permanence. One reflects on all of this, entering, perhaps the most beautiful temple in Illinois. One is electrified with its symmetry, it buttressed walls, glorious windows and the illustrious altar. Broadway Presbyterian Church in Rock Island, Illinois, reminds one of Longfellow's "The Builders."

> "In the elder years of art
> Builders wrought with greatest care
> Each minute and hidden part,
> For the gods see everywhere."

In St. Paul's cathedral in London, over the tomb of Christopher Wren, we read the memorial, "If you seek his monument, look about you." Today, we remember William Stuhr in this sanctuary of unexcelled beauty because of his soul that was akin to God, a master workman with aspirations toward eternal beauty.

Mr. William Stuhr

June 27, 1968 in Broadway Presbyterian Church,
Rock Island, Illinois

Sermonette

In all ages, reflective minds have brooded long over the concealment of nature and the silence of God. Clouds and

124

darkness surround God's throne. Man's origin has been made obscure, likewise the beginning of his thought, language, and morals. Nature has also clouded man's tomb. What we call the realm of death is one of the imponderables. Nature hides behind the walls of granite. Man has discovered some of nature's secrets. Man, of whom Bryant wrote in "Thanatopsis": "To him, who in the love of nature, holds communion with her visible forms," has found how to make the bitter sweet, the hard metal soft, the desert to blossom as a garden, and how to harness lightning, atomic energy, and gravitation to his will. With all our discoveries, the one secret unrevealed is the grave. Tears, prayer, desires, will not reveal that secret. All feet, walking the path of eminence and glory, or the path of obscurity, end in the unknown and unknowable. Shakespeare says: "We travel over the level of time to the undiscovered country from which no traveler returns." Youth may say, "Man is fashioned like a god," but age echoes, "Man is a fading leaf." Yet, man's thoughts outnumber the sands, his hopes exceed the stars, and his friendships are beyond measurement. His ambition outlasts the allotted three score and ten years, "'making our human life sublime, with memories of His sacred might.'"

A stranger knocked at Wordsworth's door and asked if the poet was in his library. The aged servant pointed to the lake and hills and said, "His library is out-of-doors." And it was, as he wrote, "Nature never did betray the heart that loved her." Nature's architect is God. The earth is His great cathedral. It is light of the sun, raiment of clouds, choirs of singing brooks, altars of pure spotless snow, and roofs of shining stars. "The heavens declare the glory of God and the firmament showeth His handiwork." When Bryant saw the water-fowl pursuing its way through the rosy sky, he exclaimed:

"He, Who from zone to zone
Guides through the boundless sky that certain flight,
In the long way that I must tread alone
Will lead my steps aright."

We do not know the way but we know God. What God has ordained must be eternal. The paintings of Leonardo da Vinci endure; can we say the artist will die? The dreams of Shakespeare are immortal; can we say the author is mortal and will die? The words of St. Paul outlast centuries; can we say the apostle died? When one lives exclusively in the material world with carnal wishes and coarse desires, why should he ask for immortality? But build with God as a co-laborer, and annihilation is contrary to our terms.

God provides things in the rough and man refines them with his arts. From cave to hut, to palace, to cathedral, man with architectural design refines his structure by refining his soul. The supreme architectural structure is the temple. The temple ministers to the spiritual needs and never dies.

In Soloman's temple were two pillars, "Jachin" for strength and "Boaz" for beauty. On the top of the pillars was lily work. We honor God with strength and beauty and with lily work. Outward beauty is a reflection of inner aspirations. The soul is more majestic than any cathedral if it is in tune with the universe. Perfection, of course, is pursuit, not possession. In building, principles are the foundation stones; habits are the columns and pillars; faculties are the master builders; thoughts are driven nails; deeds make strong the timbers; holy aspirations add color and light; imagination lends beauty to the ceiling. The beauty of which I speak is not veneer, it has internal quality; it is not made by hands but is eternal in the heavens. Where there is beauty there is holiness, and where there is holiness there is beauty. Ugliness is error, and error is a form of sin.

We enter this sanctuary with its order, symmetry, design, harmony, and balance. We stand on holy ground. The aesthetic appeal brings thought too deep for words. The arches reach from earth to heaven and from heaven back to earth. It is sinful in the atmosphere to be irreverent in thought, mediocre in desire, or lacking in appreciation for conscious beauty. Emerson said, "If eyes were made for seeing, then beauty is its own excuse for being."

What more can one say? Mr. Stuhr has said it, not in words, but in deeds. Edward Young writes, "The soul of man was made to walk the skies."

"Build thee more stately mansions, O my soul,
As the swift seasons roll!
Leave thy low-vaulted past!
Let each new temple, nobler than the last,
Shut thee from heaven with a dome more vast,
Till thou at length art free,
Leaving thine outgrown shell by life's unresting sea!"

Mr. Stuhr built this holy temple to God, for God built a holy temple within him. A man who can look back upon such a life can afford to await the end of life with calmness. He hath done what he could and hath done it well. He awaited the end assured that no harm could befall him. He had given to life his best, and there was in his soul the implicit faith that life cannot return evil for good. The strongest argument for immortality is the worth of this present life, and the value and meaning of man's soul. In fact, it is not immortality that Christ taught, it is eternal life. It is quality not quantity. It is a question of values that warrant continued life after death. Like Mr. Stuhr, we are going to seek fullness and richness of life as we now live it. We shall seek to put every possible value into the present life. "Where thy treasure is, there will thy heart be also." The soul that is devoted to things of value, beautiful things, great things, will carry with it into the future a life that is full and rich, endowed with treasures laid up in heaven. Emerson expresses it:

"What is excellent,
As God lives, is permanent
Hearts are dust, hearts' loves remain
Heart's love will meet thee again."

Death is an incident in man's soul life. It is not a stopping point, it is a stepping point. It is a natural transition from a material sphere to a spiritual one. Some say it is "from time into eternity." That cannot be. Time is itself a part of eternity. Therefore we are now in eternity as much as we shall be. If we live right, we die right, and the less we have to question about the future. We remember one who added strength to beauty and this is the preparation we follow—as we join in turning the discords of life into harmony, the ugliness into beauty—and the temple of man into the city whose Builder and Maker is God.

Mr. Stuhr's soul was made to walk the skies.

(The following thoughts by Mrs. McKenzie upon the conclusion of the Interim Pastorate in Broadway Church were also a tribute to Mr. Stuhr.)

"To Broadway Church"

In this sacred shrine
Your hours of worship
Have been shared with us.
Born in the soul of an artist,
The beauty of this temple—
Your inspiration through the years,
Is now a treasure to be tightly held
Among our memories.

Your welcome and appreciation
Have warmed us in their gracious glow;
Reflecting in our efforts
A joy in service
Which likewise will be remembered,
When we shall recall
The many happy hours spent
In this place.

Sad at leaving friends we love,
Yet we will gladly hear
Of zeal and courage
You will bring
To challenges that lie beyond.
Our prayer is for your glorious growth
To match the rich influence and tradition
Through past years.